THE *Serendipity* EFFECT

LARRY VERSTRAETE

Cover by Brian Boyd

Scholastic-TAB Publications Ltd.

Scholastic-TAB Publications Ltd.
123 Newkirk Road, Richmond Hill, Ontario, Canada L4C 3G5

Scholastic Inc.
730 Broadway, New York, NY 10003, USA

Ashton Scholastic Limited
165 Marua Road, Panmure, PO Box 12328, Auckland 6, New
Zealand

Ashton Scholastic Pty Limited
PO Box 579, Gosford, NSW 2250, Australia

Scholastic Publications Ltd.
Holly Walk, Leamington Spa, Warwickshire CV32 4LS,
England

Canadian Cataloguing in Publication Data
Verstraete, Larry
The serendipity effect

ISBN 0-590-71889-4

1.Serendipity in science - Juvenile literature.
I. Title.

Q172.5.S47V47 1989   j500   C88-095030-7

9 8 7 6 5 4 3 2   Printed in Canada   0 1 2 3 4 5/9
Manufactured by Webcom Limited

For Jo, Stephen and Ashley

Contents

Introduction

What triggers the brainstorm that leads to a scientific discovery? What stirs an inventor to create something new, to see possibilities never seen before?

Ideas surface in the strangest ways, often when they are least expected. Sometimes they seem to pop up almost by accident.

The story of James Hargreaves' invention is a good example:

In the eighteenth century, the only way to spin wool into thread was with a hand-operated spinning wheel. The job was a tedious one and produced only one thread at a time. Hargreaves, a weaver and carpenter, looked for ways to make the spinning wheel more efficient.

He was thinking about this one day while he watched someone use a spinning wheel. Suddenly the spinning wheel was knocked over. As it lay on its side, the wheel continued to turn and so did the spindle or shaft on which the thread was wound. But instead of being in horizontal position, parallel to the ground, the spindle was now in a vertical position, sticking straight up in the air.

The accident gave Hargreaves an idea. If the spindle was set in an upright position, more than one could be used at a time. Several threads could be spun at the same time.

By 1764 Hargreaves had developed a machine with upright spindles that could spin thread five times faster than by hand. He called it the spinning jenny after his daughter Jenny.

A toppled spinning wheel had spurred James Hargreaves to action. A simple accident led to important changes in the clothing industry.

Of course, serious scientists and inventors don't *depend* on accidents for success. But mistakes, mishaps, unusual coincidences and strange twists of luck happen all the time. Occasionally such surprises can be helpful. Sometimes they provide new and valuable information, point out solutions to problems or open the doors of imagination, making the impossible suddenly seem possible.

Fate has often played a part in science and invention. In fact we even have a word to describe it. The ability to make unexpected discoveries by accident is called *serendipity*.

This book is about the errors, accidents, coincidences and odd circumstances that have started or changed the discovery process. It is about the inventions and breakthroughs, old and new, large and small, that are in some way due to the serendipity effect.

New Perspectives

Have any of these things ever happened to you?

- You fill a basin with water. Then you put something in it and water sloshes all over the floor.

- You find a chunk of food that's been lying around too long. It's covered with disgusting mold.

- You're in a hurry and you have to jot down a list. You can't find a pencil or pen anywhere — so you use a wax crayon.

- After a hike in the woods you discover burrs stuck all over your clothes.

It's likely you've had at least one of these experiences. And it's equally likely that you've never given it a second thought.

Perhaps you should ...

Sometimes a perfectly ordinary experience can unexpectedly trigger a totally new idea!

Believe it or not, each of the events just mentioned sparked a startling scientific discovery or an exciting invention. Read on.

Pythagoras
About 540 B.C.

A Blacksmith's Pounding

About twenty-five hundred years ago, a Greek scholar named Pythagoras turned an everyday incident into a major discovery that completely changed the field of music.

One day Pythagoras was wandering through the streets of Crotone in southern Italy. He passed a blacksmith at work in the doorway of his shop. Pythagoras stopped to watch the man pound and shape horseshoes on different anvils. Each time the blacksmith brought his hammer down, a loud *clang* filled the air.

At first the sounds seemed ordinary enough. But then Pythagoras' keen senses noticed something else. Whenever the blacksmith switched anvils, the sounds changed — the tones were different. His curiosity aroused, Pythagoras pondered the problem as he continued on his way.

At home Pythagoras stretched a piece of string between two wooden pegs on a board. He plucked the string and heard a musical twang. When he used a longer string, he heard a lower, deeper twang.

By changing the lengths of strings, Pythagoras made an interesting discovery. The longer the string, the lower the tone. The shorter the string, the higher the tone.

But Pythagoras was just beginning his experiments. He chose a string and tied it taut to the board. Next to it he fastened a string twice its length. When he plucked both strings together, he found that they produced a pleasing combination of notes. Because one string was exactly twice as long as the other, their mathematical ratio was 2 to 1.

When Pythagoras used a string that was one and a half times as long as the first, he produced another pleasing combination of notes. This time the ratio of lengths was 3 to 2.

Over and over, Pythagoras changed the lengths of strings and compared the musical notes he made. He found that the most harmonious or pleasant sounds were made when the lengths were in small ratios to each other — 2 to 1, 3 to 2, 4 to 3. When he tried more complicated ratios — 19 to 9 or 23 to 13 — the sound combinations were unpleasant to listen to.

Pythagoras had discovered that there is a predictable numerical pattern to the most pleasing musical sounds. By applying his mathematical ratios, he could compose a whole range of harmonious notes.

Over the years, the connections between music and mathematics have been studied even further. Nowadays, all musical instruments — string, wind and bass — use the simple ratios discovered by Pythagoras many centuries ago.

Archimedes
About 250 B.C.

An Overfilled Bath

Over two thousand years ago the most feared force on earth was the powerful Roman army. Yet when the mighty Roman troops set out to crush the Greek city of Syracuse, they were almost flattened by the brilliant inventions of a single man.

Imagine huge catapults heaving enormous boulders, mechanical cranes that seized and overturned entire ships, and massive lenses which focused the sun's rays on enemy vessels, setting them on fire!

For their time, they were truly awesome, but to Archimedes, the inventor of these weapons, they were mere toys, objects for his amusement. Today Archimedes is remembered for more than his warlike creations.

By all accounts, Archimedes was a deep thinker. Often hours flew by as he pondered a problem. Then he would suddenly announce a solution, as though the answer had just popped into his head! Perhaps the famous story of the king's crown is the best example.

King Hieron II of Syracuse had ordered a new crown made out of solid gold. The finished article was beautiful, but Hieron was suspicious. He thought that maybe the goldsmith had mixed silver in with the gold. Hieron asked Archimedes if he could find out the truth for him without damaging the crown.

Archimedes pondered the problem. Silver is less dense than gold and therefore weighs less. That much he knew. The obvious thing to do, then, was to weigh the crown and then weigh an equal amount of pure gold to see if their weights were the same.

The question was, how to measure the precise amount of metal that had gone into the making of the crown? The only sure-fire method that Archimedes could think of was to melt it down and then to measure the volume of the molten liquid.

But he couldn't do that, because the king didn't want the crown damaged in any way.

Gradually Archimedes became more and more possessed by the problem. He lost track of time, forgetting even to eat or sleep.

Then one day he went to the public baths to relax. As he stepped into the full bath, he noticed that water spilled over the side.

To everyone else, this was just something that happened everyday. But to Archimedes, suddenly it was the solution to his problem!

In that instant he realized that the amount of spilled or displaced water equalled the volume of his body as he got into the bath.

Archimedes leaped out of the bath — so excited he didn't even get dressed — ran out of the building and down the street shouting "Eureka! Eureka!" (I have found it!)

As soon as he was home, he pushed the king's crown into a bowl filled to the top with water and measured the amount of liquid that spilled out, for he knew now that the volume of the water displaced by the crown would be the same as the volume of the crown itself.

Next, Archimedes measured out an equal volume of pure gold. Then he checked the weight of the pure gold against the weight of the crown, and sure enough, the crown was lighter.

The king had indeed been cheated.

The goldsmith was punished; Archimedes was rewarded; and the world was given a way to establish the relative density and purity of different materials, a method we still use two thousand years later.

Galileo Galilei
1581

The Swinging Chandelier

It was a typical Sunday in 1581. Hundreds of worshippers filled the huge cathedral in Pisa, Italy. Most of them listened intently to the church service.

But not seventeen-year-old Galileo Galilei. Instead, he kept his eyes on a chandelier overhead. Air currents flowing through the lofty cathedral moved the chandelier from side to side, back and forth. Sometimes it moved gently; sometimes it swung in a wide arc. No matter what the size of its swing, it seemed to Galileo that the chandelier kept steady time.

They didn't have clocks or watches in those days, so Galileo felt for the pulse in his wrist. He timed the chandelier's swing with his pulse beats. One, two, three beats for one swing. One, two, three beats for another swing.

Galileo was surprised. No matter how wide or narrow the swing, it always took the same number of pulse beats.

Right after the service, Galileo raced home. Quickly he suspended a weight from a long string. Galileo pulled the weight back a short distance, released it and timed its swing. He tried it again, this time pulling the weight back farther before releasing it. After many tries, Galileo had confirmed his suspicions — the time it took to make one swing was always the same, whether the swing was wide or narrow. Galileo had discovered the principle of the pendulum.

Galileo tried some experiments with his pendulum. He discovered that the length of string, amount of weight and other factors all had some predictable relationship to the time of a pendulum's swing.

Some years later, Galileo wanted to do some experimenting with falling objects, but he found he had a problem. How could he accurately time something that moved so rapidly?

Then he remembered the pendulum. The weight of the pendulum acted just like a falling object — except it didn't fall straight down. It fell on a slant and at a slower rate that could be timed easily.

Galileo adapted the pendulum as a timepiece. First he got a wooden board and carved a long, straight, smooth groove down the centre. When he raised the board slightly at one end and released a ball, it slowly rolled down the groove.

Galileo marked off his grooved board into small divisions of equal length. As a timing device he used a water-filled container with a small hole in the bottom. By counting water drops, he could keep track of time. Now he was ready to begin.

He released one ball at a time from the higher end of the board. As it rolled, Galileo timed how long it took to cross each division of the board. To his amazement, Galileo discovered that the balls didn't travel down the track at an even rate. Instead, they speeded up — or accelerated — as they got farther down the groove. Falling objects, he found, picked up speed as they fell to the earth.

After more experiments, Galileo was able to work out a mathematical formula to help him calculate the acceleration of a falling object. To prove his point, he even predicted how far a cannonball could be fired from a cannon.

In many ways the swinging chandelier started a revolution in the world of science. Galileo proved that measurement and experimentation could be used to check out observations, to prove a natural law beyond a shadow of a doubt. And so he began the experimental process scientists — and science students — still use today!

William Lee
1589

Noisy Needles

Click, clack ... click, clack ...

In the sixteenth century, this was a common sound in many English homes. It was the sound of metal hitting metal, needle striking needle as women in each household sat evening after evening knitting clothes they were too poor to buy.

It was the same in the home of Reverend William Lee, a church minister. One night Mrs. Lee sat by the fireplace knitting while her husband dreamily watched her work. Her hands flew over the needles as she formed one stitch after another. First she made a loop with the wool, then she pulled another loop through the first one. Loop, pull, loop, pull. Over and over she repeated the process.

Suddenly, an idea popped into Lee's head. He sat straight up. Why not make a machine to repeat those tedious steps? Think how much easier and faster knitting would be!

Lee built a wooden frame with hundreds of small needles and a series of hooks that lifted loops over the wool. With one simple action, the operator of this knitting machine could knit a whole row of stitches at one time!

Lee spent the remainder of his life trying to interest people in his invention, but not many people bought his machine. He died in 1610, penniless and disappointed.

His brother later managed to sell the idea to some merchants, and soon afterwards, a frame-knitting factory opened in England. For the first time, knitted clothes could be produced cheaply and quickly. William Lee's invention opened the door to the machine age.

Hans Lippershey
About 1600

Close Enough to Touch

Many different stories have been told about the invention of the telescope. The one about Hans Lippershey has never been disproved, and may well be true.

Lippershey was a maker of eyeglasses in Middlepoint, Holland, early in the seventeenth century. One day he was standing in the doorway of his shop polishing some lenses he had just made. It was his custom to hold the finished lenses up to the light. That way he could see flaws in the glass more easily. Absentmindedly, he held the two lenses up to the light and looked through both at the same time.

The church tower in the distance seemed to leap out at him! Lippershey was so startled he almost dropped his lenses. When he calmed down, he held up the lenses and looked at the tower again. Sure enough, the tower appeared to be close enough to touch.

Lippershey noticed that he had used two different lenses. The one closest to his eye was concave or curved inward on one side. The lens closest to the tower was convex or curved outward on one side. By moving the lenses closer or farther apart he could focus the image of the tower clearly.

At first Hans Lippershey simply thought

that he had invented an interesting toy. He mounted the lenses on a board so his customers could view the church tower in the distance. Soon his invention became very popular around town and his business boomed!

Eventually he refined his device. He enclosed the lenses in an adjustable hollow tube. He called it his *kijkglas* ("look glass").

On October 2, 1608, Lippershey applied for a patent for his "look glass" so that he would be the only person allowed to produce and sell his invention. He was refused. The government told him that his idea was not completely original for "too many people have knowledge of this invention."

It seems that other lens grinders in Holland had applied for patents on similar inventions at about the same time as Hans Lippershey.

Exactly who discovered this trick with the lenses — and *how* it was discovered — may always be a mystery, but Lippershey's accidental discovery may well have led the way to the beginnings of the telescope, binoculars and microscopes we use today!

Alois Senefelder
1798

A Hurried List

It was an ordinary, quickly jotted laundry list that gave Alois Senefelder his idea — and it turned out to be one of the most important advances in the history of printing.

Have you ever done potato printing? If you take a firm potato, carve a design into it, ink it using a stamp pad and then press it onto paper, you will get a printed copy of your design. Only it won't be *exactly* the same. The print will be the reverse of your potato design.

In the 1700s, they used a very similar procedure to reproduce pictures. A printing plate — a metal, wood or stone version of the potato carving — was prepared through engraving or etching. An engraving was made by carving the picture in reverse on wood or soft metal. In etching, the reverse design was sketched in pencil on a metal sheet or on limestone, and then strong chemicals were used to gouge or etch parts of the metal. By using either engraving or etching, the printer had an image that was ready to be inked.

Alois Senefelder was fascinated with the etching process. He was naturally an inquisitive and ambitious person, and he began to experiment with inks and chemicals in order to improve this method of printing.

To help earn extra money, Alois' mother ran a small laundry business. One day in 1798, after being swamped with orders, she asked Alois to help her. Would he write down the orders before she forgot them? Alois quickly searched for pencil and paper. But he couldn't find any. He grabbed the nearest tools he could find — a polished limestone slab and a greasy crayon he had just invented. Hurriedly he scribbled the laundry list on the limestone.

At the very moment he was writing, Alois had a brainstorm. Knowing that grease and water don't mix, he quickly poured watery acid over the stone, covering it. While most of the slab stayed wet with the solution, the parts on which he had written with greasy crayon instantly repelled the acid, and stayed dry.

Then Alois poured oil-based ink on the limestone. It ran off the wet areas and stayed on the grease. Hardly able to contain his excitement, he quickly pressed the inked slab on paper.

To his surprise, he had printed a reverse image of the laundry list!

Alois Senefelder had discovered a printing process much simpler and more accurate than either etching or engraving. It became known as lithography — *litho* for "stone" and *graphy* for "writing" — and is still used by printers all over the world.

A Moldy Potato

Today we all know that micro-organisms or bacteria cause diseases. By controlling the spread of bacteria, we can control the spread of disease.

In the late 1800s, though, this was a brand new idea, and many people didn't believe it. How could something too tiny to be seen by the unaided eye, actually cause a disease?

Robert Koch, a German scientist, did not believe that the idea was ridiculous at all. He spent long hours in his laboratory in Berlin trying to isolate and study bacteria.

One day in 1880, while he was cleaning up his laboratory, Koch noticed a piece of boiled potato someone had left on the table. The potato had been lying there for a few days, and was already covered with furry mold.

Koch picked up the potato and was about to throw it away when suddenly he stopped and looked closely at it. Wasn't *this* interesting?

Robert Koch had seen moldy food before. But this time he noticed that the mold grew in patches. And each separate patch was a different colour!

Koch pulled a bit of gray mold off the potato. He put it on a glass slide, added a drop of water, and looked at it under his microscope. He saw a swarm of bacteria that all looked alike.

When he examined the red patch he saw a different kind of micro-organism. Each colored patch he found, contained a cluster of a separate type of bacteria. Each patch was a colony that had started from a single micro-organism.

This meant that if a single micro-organism was placed on a suitable food source, it would grow and multiply to become a colony of identical bacteria.

Robert Koch's second glance at a simple potato gave scientists a way to grow and isolate bacteria for study. It was the beginning of the science of bacteriology and the end of many diseases!

Folding Chairs on Wheels

If you went grocery shopping before 1937, you needed a sturdy back and strong arm muscles. As you roamed the aisles, you would pile your groceries into baskets and bags that you had to lug around the store with you. Strenuous exercise!

Sylvan N. Goldman of Oklahoma City was in the supermarket business. He figured that there had to be an easier way to shop.

One night in 1936, he sat on a folding chair in his small office thinking about this problem. How could he make shopping more convenient and less exhausting? He toyed around with several plans, but none of them was very good. Then, as he glanced at his chair, he suddenly had a whopper of an idea! Later he said "Inspiration hit me right between the eyes."

He placed two folding chairs together and looked at them. It would work! If he joined the chairs and added wheels underneath and a basket on top, Goldman figured that he would have an easy-to-push cart. Like the chairs, the cart could be folded for convenient storage too.

On June 4, 1937, Goldman's first batch of shopping carts was ready for use in his store. But the day was a disappointment. Instead of excitedly using the carts, customers avoided the new invention. They thought that if they used a cart, people would think they were weak!

Then Goldman had another great idea. He hired some people to push the carts around his store, pretending to be shoppers. It wasn't long before real customers copied the phony customers.

Sylvan Goldman's grocery carts have made grocery shopping a breeze for billions of customers since 1937. Today tens of millions of shopping carts are used in stores around the world.

Sticky Burrs

Last time you hiked in the woods, you probably collected burrs or tiny seed pods on your clothing. These prickly travelling seeds stick firmly and are a nuisance to pry loose. Yet it was the humble burr that inspired George de Mestral to create a marvellous invention.

By day George de Mestral managed a small machine shop in Nyon, Switzerland. In his spare time he invented things. His inventions were practical, but not one of them was wildly successful. All that changed after an innocent encounter with annoying, clinging burrs.

One day in 1948, de Mestral went on a hunting trip. As he wound his way over mountain trails, tiny burrs stuck to his socks and trousers. He stopped to pry off the sticky seeds, but found it was no easy task. Each burr clung stubbornly to his clothes and freeing them took a lot of effort and patience.

George de Mestral was curious. Just why were the burrs so hard to remove? When he looked at the burrs up close, he noticed that each one had tiny hooks that latched on to the loops of thread in his clothing. His inventive mind began to churn. Why not make a fastener of loops and hooks that locked on to one another?

The idea was far simpler than the process.

To make the fastener work, de Mestral needed two types of cloth — one with hooks, the other with loops. After some searching he found a weaver who would make the cloth by hand on a small loom.

De Mestral eagerly tried out the first sample. It worked! The hooks locked into the loops. But to manufacture the fastener in bulk, a quicker method had to be found.

De Mestral experimented with many techniques — steam, hot air, ultrasonic sound, glue. After months of trial and error he found a way of making rigid loops of nylon thread. But he still did not know how to make the hooks.

De Mestral retreated to a mountain cabin to ponder the problem. Several days later, he had an idea. On the way down the mountain, he stopped to buy a pair of barber's clippers. Then he visited a friend who was a loom-maker. He showed his friend how to use the clippers to cut the rigid loops. Once cut, the loops became hooks. George de Mestral and his friend then built a special loom to weave the loops and then cut them into hooks.

About eight years had passed since de Mestral had had his brainstorm on the mountain. Finally George de Mestral had his fastener of loops and hooks, and a machine that could make it quickly. He called his fastener Velcro — Vel for velvet, cro for "crochet" or small hook in French.

With Velcro, parts can be joined and separated quickly and easily, time and time again. Today it has hundreds of uses, from replacing snaps, buttons and zippers in clothes and running shoes to attaching gear in space shuttles.

Fortunate Fumbles

Smashed bottles, sudden explosions, jarring jolts of electricity, spilled chemicals!

Can such accidents ever really lead to great inventions?

Consider the case of the Philadelphia soda-fountain attendant. When he scooped out a serving of ice cream for a customer in 1874, he couldn't have known that an accident would put him on the brink of a new taste discovery!

At that time, soda fountains were popular places. Friends met there to enjoy ice cream and a "soda," a drink invented by Joseph Priestly in the 1700s. To make a soda, carbon dioxide gas was passed through distilled water, and then mixed with whichever sweet, flavored syrups the customer chose.

On this day, the Philadelphia attendant was serving up a scoop of ice cream when the ice cream slipped off the spoon and splashed into a glass of soda. The fizzy, creamy mixture looked so tasty that the attendant tried it. It was delicious! Before long ice cream sodas were a hit at soda fountains across the country.

As you'll see in the following stories, an accident that at first seems disastrous may, in fact, be an opportunity in disguise.

Berthold Schwartz
About 1350

An Explosive Mix

When a story gets passed on from person to person some of the details change. After a while it is difficult to tell just how true the tale is. That's why the story behind one of the most exciting inventions remains so mysterious.

From all accounts the inventor was a monk named Berthold Schwartz, who lived in Freiburg, Germany, in the fourteenth century. Berthold liked to experiment with different chemicals, crushing and stirring them together to form new mixtures. Often he made healing potions for the peasants who lived near the monastery.

One day Berthold was busy making medicine. The ingredients were three readily available chemicals — sulfur, charcoal and sodium nitrite. After he had ground them into fine powders, he mixed them together. Then he placed a stone on top of the container to act as a loose-fitting lid.

Later, when Berthold went to light a fire, he struck a flint. By chance a few sparks flew into the container setting the mixture on fire. It exploded with a *bang*, hurling the stone upward with so much force that it smashed right through the roof!

Quite by accident Berthold Schwartz had

discovered gunpowder, one of the earliest explosives.

Fortunately the monk wasn't hurt in the accident. He wasn't even scared! Instead, he was fascinated by the explosive. He mixed up more batches of the powders and ignited them. The peaceful monastery rocked with explosion after explosion.

Later Berthold made an iron tube that was closed at one end except for a small hole. He stuffed gunpowder into the tube and put a stone ball on top of the open end. Then he touched a flame to the small hole. The mixture exploded, shooting out the stone ball with great force. Berthold had made the first simple gun.

Berthold Schwartz changed the face of history. Not only did he make a weapon that could shoot things great distances but he also produced a powerful explosive strong enough to blast rocks out of the earth. At last men had a tool that could move mountains!

**Pieter van Muschenbroeck
1746**

A Jar of Electricity

Have you ever walked across a carpeted floor and then touched a doorknob or a friend? That small jolt, or shock, you received is the discharge of static electricity, and it is created by friction.

This effect has been known for centuries. Over two hundred years ago it was popular to build friction machines or electrostatic generators to produce static electricity. You could crank a handle on a generator and produce an electric charge. When some daring person touched the machine, they got a tiny jolt of discharged electricity!

The problem with electrostatic generators was that they couldn't store up electricity. Once discharged by a touch, the charge was gone, and the machine would have to be cranked again to produce another charge.

In 1746, a professor at the University of Leyden in Holland tried to make a device that would hold electricity. Professor Pieter van Muschenbroeck and two assistants thought that they could capture an electrical charge if they could somehow surround an electrified object with a non-conductor — such as glass.

They hooked up an electrostatic generator to a brass chain, which they dangled inside a glass jar. When they cranked the generator, electricity flowed down the chain to the jar. But when they touched a conductor to the jar, nothing happened. The electricity, it seemed, had disappeared.

The professor tried another approach. This time he filled the jar with water, again hooked up the chain to the machine and cranked the handle. But once again it seemed that they had failed.

Discouraged, they began to dismantle the machine. An assistant held the jar with one hand while the water inside was still connected to the generator. With his other hand he grabbed the wire to remove it from the machine. All of a sudden a jolt of electricity surged through his body, paralyzing his arms and legs!

The jar had indeed stored electricity. By touching the wire and the jar at the same time, the man had acted as a shortcut for the electrical charges. After a few hours, he recovered.

The apparatus became known as a Leyden jar. In it strong currents could be stored for a long time, enabling scientists to discover many new properties and benefits of electricity.

Benjamin Franklin
1750

Christmas Party of a Different Sort

Look in almost any history book about the eighteenth century and you'll be sure to find the name Benjamin Franklin. He was a famous statesman, doctor and newspaper man as well as an outstanding inventor and scientist.

One of Franklin's passions was electricity. Little was known about this force in the 1750s, but Franklin opened the door to its wonders.

From the moment Benjamin Franklin saw his first Leyden jar, he was intrigued by the device. It didn't take him long to improve it either. By lining the jar inside and out with metal instead of filling it with water, he was able to contain larger electrical charges for longer periods of time. Figuring that the jar's shape was not a crucial factor, Franklin took several large panes of glass, coated them on both sides with metal, hooked up wires and ran electricity into them. This way he could hold even larger charges than before. By connecting several Leyden jars together he could even produce a charge strong enough to kill a small animal.

According to one story, Franklin invited some friends to a Christmas dinner party in 1750. His guests were surprised to find a series of Leyden jars and a live turkey at Franklin's party. Being a bit of a showman, Franklin planned to charge up the Leyden jars, then astound his friends by using an electrical shock to kill the turkey for dinner!

Everything was ready. The jars were charged. The unfortunate turkey waited nearby. Then Benjamin Franklin made a mistake.

He began to talk to one of his guests. Without thinking, he leaned against one of the jars. A huge spark lit up the room as a jolt of electricity raced through his body! The shock knocked him to the floor.

After recovering, Franklin recalled the bang and spark of the discharge. How very much like lightning and thunder, he thought. He wondered if lightning was, in fact, a huge jolt of electricity.

Franklin was eager to test his theory. He built a kite and hung from it an iron wire to attract the lightning. For string he used twine, a weak conductor. At the end of the twine he tied a silk ribbon, a non-conductor. Between the twine and the ribbon he fastened a key.

During the next thunderstorm Franklin launched his kite. As soon as the kite was struck by lightning, Franklin touched the key. There was a spark and he felt a small electrical shock. He was right! Lightning was indeed electricity. Furthermore, the electricity could move from one place to another.

Franklin discovered something else from his mishap with the turkey. Since his body had been a conductor and acted as an easy route for an electrical discharge, he figured that other conductors should be able to do the same thing. So he ran a wire from the roof of his house to the ground. Instead of lightning striking his roof now, it struck the wire and was safely diverted to the ground. Franklin had created the first lightning rod, a device we use even today.

Charred Rubber

For most of his life, Charles Goodyear was obsessed with rubber. The springy, stretchy stuff was both a blessing and a curse for the inventor. Over the years rubber provided Goodyear with recognition and glory — as well as poverty and defeat.

Goodyear's fascination with rubber started quite by accident. One day in 1834, the unemployed salesman noticed a rubber life-preserver on display in the window of a New York shop. He examined it carefully and found a defect in the product. He raced home, designed a new valve for the preserver and in a few days returned to the shop.

He was sure the manufacturer would buy his new invention. But Goodyear was wrong. The problem with the life preserver, he was told, was not the valve. It was the rubber. Despite all its wonderful elastic abilities, rubber had drawbacks too. In cold weather it became so brittle it shattered into pieces; in hot weather it became sticky and foul-smelling. Find a way around those problems, the manufacturer told Goodyear, and his company would pay a fortune for the secret.

From that time on, Charles Goodyear was hooked on rubber. With the little money he had, he bought big chunks of it. He shredded it into tiny bits, loaded the pieces into pans, added chemicals, then stirred and heated the mixtures over his kitchen stove. Later he nailed these different rubber samples all around his house to see what effect temperature had on them.

For five years Goodyear devoted himself to his experiments. He grew tired, pale and sick. Gradually his house emptied as, one at a time, he sold his household goods so he could buy food and clothing for his family and, of course, more rubber for his experiments.

Time and time again, Charles Goodyear came up with a rubber product that he believed was new and improved. He would eagerly tell everyone — family, friends, even reporters — about his discovery. Losing no time, he would rent an abandoned rubber factory and begin to manufacture products using his new formula. For a while things would roll along smoothly and then, as always, customers would begin to return his products when they discovered the defects.

Despite all the failures, Goodyear never gave up hope. Then, unexpectedly, in 1839, a small accident changed his life. He was experimenting one day with a batch of rubber, sulfur and white lead. As he stirred the mixture, a bit of it splashed onto the hot stove. Instead of melting, as Goodyear expected, it sizzled and charred around the edges. Curious about this strange reaction, Goodyear dropped another glob onto the stove. This time he could see a thin rim of rubber between the charred edge and the rest of the material. He found that this rim was flexible and moldable, like rubber, but didn't become brittle when cold or sticky when warm. Goodyear had almost solved the problem. He named his discovery 'vulcanized rubber' after Vulcan, the Roman god of fire.

Goodyear had stumbled upon the right combination of chemicals to make vulcanized rubber. And that one small spill on his stove showed him that heat was necessary — but exactly *how much* heat? Goodyear didn't know. For the next five years he experimented constantly in the family kitchen, trying to find the answer. His health worsened and his family became poorer as he struggled to finance his work.

Perhaps the ridicule Goodyear had to endure was worse than poor health and poverty. *No one* took him seriously. After all, he had failed repeatedly before. Now people laughed when he claimed that heat, the thing that made rubber sticky, was necessary to cure that stickiness.

Finally, after ten years of struggle and misfortune, his process worked. He could prove it.

But even though Goodyear received a patent for his vulcanized rubber, he did not get the wealth or respect he deserved. Other people claimed that they had invented vulcanized rubber first.

Goodyear continued to experiment on his own, developing many new uses for rubber. He sold his secrets to manufacturers. While they reaped huge profits, though, Charles Goodyear remained poor most of his life.

Today we take rubber for granted. We find it in hundreds of useful products, from erasers to surgical equipment in hospitals — thanks to the persistence and curiosity of Charles Goodyear.

Spilled Liquid

Alfred Nobel had a personal interest in explosives. His brother had been killed in a tragic accident with nitroglycerine at their explosives factory in Sweden.

In those days nitroglycerine was widely used for blasting rocks in mines and quarries. But this highly unstable liquid often exploded unexpectedly — all it took was a slight jiggle of its container!

Alfred Nobel was determined to find a safer way to use nitroglycerine. He found that if nitroglycerine was mixed with a porous white powder called kieselguhr, it could be rolled into sticks that could be carried safely anywhere. He called his new explosive dynamite.

With Nobel's discovery a powerful explosive force was locked in an easy-to-use, safe form. Before long dynamite was used widely in all areas of construction, from building roads to blasting tunnels in mines. Alfred Nobel became a wealthy man, and he opened up dynamite factories across Europe.

Nobel continued his research. One day in 1875, while experimenting with nitroglycerine, he accidentally cut his finger. Quickly he reached for a bottle of collodion and dabbed some on his finger. Collodion was often used on cuts because it dried quickly to form an elastic "skin" that sealed the wound.

As Nobel continued to work with the nitroglycerine a little of it dropped on the collodion. Much to his surprise, the collodion changed in appearance. A new gummy substance formed.

Acting on a hunch, Nobel tried some different experiments. He found that when a mixture of nitroglycerine and finely divided collodion was heated, a transparent jelly-like material formed. This new chemical was an even more powerful explosive than dynamite.

Alfred Nobel called his discovery blasting gelatin. Because of his lucky accident, it is often said that "blasting gelatin was born on a man's finger and not in a test tube!"

Thomas Edison
1877

Vibrating Needle

It's hard to imagine a world without light bulbs, wax paper, fire alarms or stereo systems. Yet these and more than a thousand other inventions were pioneered by one very energetic, imaginative man — Thomas Edison.

As a youngster, Edison earned money by selling newspapers on a train. In one corner of a railway car he set up a laboratory. With every penny he could spare, Edison bought chemicals and equipment for his experiments. He read all the scientific books he could find and devoted every spare minute to inventing.

Success came to Edison at an early age. He invented a machine that told brokers the prices of stocks on the New York Stock Exchange. This invention sold so well that at the age of twenty-three, Edison was able to retire from work and devote all his time to inventing.

He set up a laboratory at Menlo Park in New Jersey and hired mechanics and chemists to assist him. Within six short years, he had more than 120 inventions to his credit.

Edison never needed much rest. He continued to work around the clock, stopping only for short catnaps. Ideas for new inventions seemed to leap out of his head. Often he saw possibilities in situations other people ignored.

In 1877, Edison invented the first phonograph (an early type of record player). There are several versions to the story and as is often the case, it is difficult to tell which one is more accurate.

According to one account, one day in 1877, Edison was hard at work on the back of a telephone panel. He tested the machine by speaking into it. His finger was close to a steel point, and as he spoke the vibrations from his voice caused the point to vibrate and prick his finger.

Most people would have patched up the wound and continued with their work. But Edison was struck by the oddity of this accident. Suddenly he had an idea. If sound could cause a needle to vibrate, then maybe the shaking needle could etch lines into a soft material. Perhaps another needle passing over these marks would cause the sound to be repeated.

Edison held a piece of heavy paper near the needle and spoke into the telephone again. When he passed the pricked paper back a second time, the needle followed the marks it had made, and Edison heard his own voice faintly repeated. Edison had the beginnings of a sound-recording system.

According to another version, the idea for the phonograph came to Edison while he worked on the telegraph. He was testing the device one day when he noticed a faint musical hum coming from the machine. Edison investigated and discovered that this unexpected sound came from a vibrating needle. He found that he could reproduce sounds by passing a needle over grooves in wax.

By any account, it was a simple hum that had led Edison to invent the marvellous "talking machine." The first phonograph had a copper cylinder, covered with tin foil, that was turned by hand. As someone spoke into a horn, a needle vibrated and cut lines into the tin foil. When the needle passed over these same marks, the voice was played back.

Today we have sophisticated stereo systems capable of turning out high quality sound. But it all goes back to a vibrating needle that nobody else would ever have noticed!

Mixed Too Long

When you mix whipping cream long enough it turns stiff and forms little peaks. When you mix cake batter it gets smoother. If you mix soap in a machine for too long it undergoes a surprising change — as a worker for the Proctor and Gamble Company discovered in 1878.

The worker had left a batch of soap to stir in a cutcher or vat while he took his lunch break. Returning late, he realized that the soap had been churning for too long. He was afraid to admit his mistake, so he shipped out the batch of soap anyway, hoping that no one would notice his error.

Was he wrong! The company soon began receiving orders for "the soap that floats." The extra stirring the soap had received over the long lunch hour had beaten air into the mixture. Instead of sinking as most bars of soap do, the new soap floated on water.

To meet the demand, the company started producing the floating soap. But they couldn't think of a suitable name for it. Then, like the soap itself, the name came almost by accident.

Harley Proctor, the son of a partner in the firm, tried to find a suitable name. "White" ... "pure" ... "floating" ... these words appealed to Harley, but didn't have the right ring to them.

One Sunday morning in church, he heard the minister quote Psalm 45:8, "From ivory palaces stringed instruments make you glad."

The word "ivory" jumped out at Harley. He christened the new product Ivory Soap, a name that is still used today for the soap that floats.

Edouard Benedictus
1903

Unbreakable Glass

In 1903 French scientist Edouard Benedictus was approaching the end of his experiment. He stirred a liquid celluloid in a glass flask. The experiment looked successful, and Benedictus was pleased.

Suddenly his hand slipped, knocking the flask to the floor. Disappointed, he stooped down to clean up the shattered glass.

What was this? Instead of shards of glass, the flask remained intact! Somehow the fragments had been held together.

Benedictus was fascinated by the strange behaviour of the glass. He sensed something unusual — an unknown property of celluloid, perhaps. He abandoned his original experiment and set off on this new trail.

Eventually, Edouard Benedictus developed safety glass, a type of glass that cracks but does not shatter. It safely stays together even when you smash it with a hammer. Today we use safety glass in many places — for car windshields, windows, doors of public buildings, even in goggles for machinists.

Opportunity Knocks

Elias Howe, Jr., was eavesdropping in a Boston machine shop one day in 1839 — and his whole life changed!

Elias worked in the shop as an assistant. On that day the owner and another worker began to argue. As their voices grew louder, Elias became distracted from his work and listened to the two men ...

"Why waste time on a knitting machine?" he heard the owner say. "Invent a sewing machine and you'll make a fortune."

To the penniless Elias — who earned only two or three dollars a week — these words seemed like magic. A fortune! — just for a machine that sewed!

These simple words fueled Elias' imagination. For years he struggled, passing one obstacle after another, until at long last he achieved his goal — he invented the first modern sewing machine.

Fate provided Elias Howe, Jr., with inspiration and opportunity. By coincidence he happened to overhear the conversation that led to his success. When he died in 1872, at the age of forty-eight, he had amassed an incredible fortune — over thirteen million dollars!

Coincidences happen to us all the time. Usually you don't notice. They don't change your life. But to an observant person, to one on the brink of change, to one facing a problem, chance events may have meaning. Sometimes merely being in the right place at the right time can be an important step in a breakthrough.

In this chapter you will see how unexpected twists of time and place became opportunities for discovery and invention.

Luigi Galvani
1786

Twitching Legs

In a fairy tale, a frog might be a handsome prince in disguise. In science, a frog just might lead to an important discovery.

About the year 1786, an Italian university teacher, Professor Luigi Galvani, was preparing to experiment with static electricity. Like other professors of his day, he used one of his rooms at home as his laboratory. His pupils gathered there for instruction.

One day, Signora Galvani sat in the room to watch her husband. At that time frogs' legs were considered a tasty treat in Europe, and Signora Galvani passed the time skinning and cutting up some dead frogs with a sharp steel knife. She laid the pieces on a zinc plate beside her.

When she was finished, Signora Galvani laid down the knife and watched the students who were waiting for Professor Galvani to arrive. The students busied themselves by cranking a nearby electrostatic generator, producing a shower of sparks.

Suddenly, from the corner of her eye, Signora Galvani noticed a movement from the dish of legs.

Astonished, she turned to watch them closely. Sure enough, the legs twitched as if they were still alive!

Surprised as she was, Signora Galvani kept her wits about her. She continued watching and soon noticed a pattern to the movements. Only those parts of the legs that touched the knife blade resting on the edge of the metal dish twitched. The twitching also seemed to happen only when sparks were produced by the nearby electrostatic machine.

When her husband came home, Signora Galvani excitedly told him of her discovery. He, too, noticed the jerking movements as sparks flew from the machine.

Professor Galvani was fascinated with this odd behaviour. For more than six years he experimented with frogs' legs. In one experiment he hung frogs from brass hooks on the iron railings that surrounded his house. The professor suspected that if sparks from an electrostatic machine could cause twitching, then lightning should have the same effect.

But Professor Galvani was in for a surprise. One bright, sunny day he noticed that when a light breeze pushed the legs against the iron railing, they twitched. There wasn't a cloud in the sky or even a hint of electricity. Now he was truly amazed!

Professor Galvani conducted several tests indoors. He laid the frogs' legs on an iron plate, and pressed the brass hook against it. The legs flinched each time.

Galvani knew that muscles in the frogs' legs

twitched when they came in contact with electricity. Now the twitching happened even when electricity was nowhere around. Galvani thought there must be a natural source of electricity inside the frog. He called it "animal electricity."

Later another Italian professor, Alessandro Volta, also investigated the twitching. He found that whenever two different metals were separated by a moist conductor, electricity was produced. The brass hook striking the iron plate produced an electric current that caused the legs to twitch.

Galvani may have been wrong when he believed that animals have a natural source of electricity, but his discoveries were valuable to other inventors. They led to the invention of the battery, a device that produces power when two metals, usually copper and zinc, are separated by a moist mixture.

**Rene Theophile Laennec
1816**

Children's Game, Doctor's Tool

If you put your ear against someone's chest, you might be able to hear the faint beating of his heart. Until 1816, that's how a doctor examined a patient's heart, but Rene Laennec, a Paris doctor, stumbled upon a better method.

One day Dr. Laennec was on his way to visit a patient. He walked along the streets, deep in thought. His patient, a young woman with heart disease, was extremely fat and Dr. Laennec wondered if he would be able to hear the sound of her heartbeat.

The sound of laughter made the doctor stop short. Several children were playing a game on a pile of old lumber. While one child pressed his ear against one end of a long wooden beam, another child tapped the other end. The children squealed with delight when they heard the sound travel through the length of board.

Later, as he was about to examine his patient at her home, Dr. Laennec recalled the children's game. Why, of course! He took a sheet of paper and rolled it into a tube. When he pressed one end of the tube against his patient's chest and listened at the other end, he could clearly hear the movements of her heart!

Dr. Laennec experimented with different materials for his listening device. Being an expert wood turner, he finally produced a cylinder of wood about 30 cm long. It was hollow in the center and had adjustable cups at each end.

Today doctors use a variation of this instrument that was inspired by a children's game. It may look different than Dr. Laennec's invention, but the stethoscope remains the simplest way for a doctor to listen to the beating heart.

William Beaumont
1822

Hole in the Stomach

William Beaumont was a dedicated army surgeon. His unit was part of a peace-keeping force the United States Army had stationed on Mackinac Island in Lake Huron, near the shores of present day Michigan. In a small village on the island, the American Fur Trading Company also maintained its headquarters.

The ambitious Dr. Beaumont felt that his talents were being wasted on the calm little island. Even at the peak of the fur trading season, few incidents called for a surgeon's skills. But then along came Alexis St. Martin — and the doctor's peaceful life was changed forever.

Alexis St. Martin was a carefree, adventure-loving French Canadian youth. He had been hired as a voyageur by the American Fur Trading Company to transport furs by canoe through the wilderness of North America. With the fur trading season drawing to a close, St. Martin, like other voyageurs, had returned to headquarters on Mackinac Island.

On June 6, 1822, St. Martin was relaxing with other men in the company store. Nearby, a drunken voyageur toyed with his newly purchased gun. Suddenly, the gun went off! A full load of buckshot and powder ripped into Alexis

St. Martin's body, just below his chest.

Within minutes Dr. Beaumont was at the youth's side. He was amazed the voyageur was still alive, for in his abdomen was a gaping hole, larger than his own hand! Part of his stomach and part of one lung poked through the cavity.

Dr. Beaumont cleaned the wound and applied a dressing. He fully expected the voyageur to die. But Alexis St. Martin did not die. His wound healed in a peculiar way. Rather than settling back into the abdomen, his stomach attached itself to the chest wall. Scar tissue formed around his wound, but the hole remained open. Only a loose flap of stomach lining hung over it like a shade pulled over a window. If you pushed aside this flap, you could see inside St. Martin's stomach!

Dr. Beaumont recognized a rare opportunity that he couldn't let slip through his fingers. He could be the first person to actually examine a living stomach, the first to discover how food is processed by the body. He would solve the mysteries of digestion.

Because St. Martin no longer had the strength or endurance to work as a voyageur, he was dependent on the doctor for food and shelter. Reluctantly, he agreed to go along with Dr. Beaumont's tests.

Dr. Beaumont began a series of well-planned and painless experiments. He tied tiny bits of food to silk threads and lowered them through the hole into St. Martin's stomach. Now and then he would lift them out, observe the state of digestion, then return them to the stomach. He extracted, analyzed and experimented with stomach juices too. Once, he even poked a thermometer through the hole to check the stomach's temperature. No one before him had ever been able to do these things.

For twelve years, Dr. Beaumont conducted experiment after experiment. His findings startled doctors and scientists and opened the doors to a new branch of science — the study of food and how the body uses it. Dr. Beaumont became a respected and admired authority across North America and Europe.

And what of Alexis St. Martin? For fifty-eight years after the accident he continued to be a medical wonder. He received dozens of invitations to appear before interested groups and show his now famous hole. The fees that he collected helped support his growing family.

Dr. Beaumont's experiments must indeed have been harmless, for Alexis St. Martin lived to the ripe old age of eighty-three, outliving the doctor by twenty-seven years!

John and Allan McIntosh
1835

Fruit From a Single Tree

Many varieties of apples are grown in Canada and the United States, but the undisputed favorite is the McIntosh Red. In these two countries alone, millions of this crisp, juicy fruit are harvested each year.

But the McIntosh Red had humble beginnings and if it wasn't for a bit of luck 150 years ago, this popular fruit might not be found in kitchens today.

In 1811, a Scottish settler named John McIntosh moved to a homestead in Dundas County, Ontario. In order to prepare the land for farming, he began clearing the trees off his property. As luck would have it, John found a cluster of 20 young apple trees hidden in the dense bush.

To the young farmer, finding the trees was as good as finding gold, for apples were a valuable commodity to pioneer settlers. The fruit added variety to an otherwise bland diet. Apples were versatile, too. They could be eaten straight off the tree in summer, stored in a cool place for the winter, cooked into cakes, pies and other delicacies or even squeezed into refreshing juice or cider.

John uprooted the young trees and transplanted them closer to his home. The following season, he had an ample supply of tasty apples. However, one of the trees produced an especially sweet and delicious fruit. It quickly became a favorite with the whole family and with neighbors from near and far.

Unfortunately, one tree could hardly produce enough fruit to satisfy one family, let alone the entire neighborhood. Although John tried planting seeds taken from the fruit, the new trees did not bear the same apples. As John soon discovered, apple trees do not "breed true." That is, seeds from the fruit do not produce apples exactly like the parent tree.

For over twenty years, the tree continued to bear fruit, but never enough to satisfy everyone. Then, one day in 1835, a wandering farmhand happened to hear the tale of the single tree with the delicious fruit. He offered to help.

Taking a sharp knife, he cut a short twig from the apple tree. Then he walked over to a young seedling tree, carved a small slit into its bark near the top, and inserted the twig. Using some twine, he wrapped it around the joint to keep it in place.

This procedure is called grafting. As the seedling grows, the twig grows too and becomes the top of the new tree. Then the new tree will bear the same fruit as the original.

The method worked. Allan, John's oldest son, began traveling around the area selling branches of the tree to other farmers. With each sale, he showed them how to graft the branches to their own apple seedlings.

The original tree on John McIntosh's farm died in 1910. By then the McIntosh Red could be found all over the continent from the United States in the south, to the fertile Okanagan Valley of British Colombia in the west, and the rich Annapolis Valley of Nova Scotia in the east.

David Fife
1843

Seeds in the Mail

A package of seeds in the mail started a chain of events that changed the face of farming in North America.

David Fife was an unusual man. Instead of planting a single crop of grain like his neighbors in Peterborough, Ontario, Fife planted many different kinds of wheat each year. His farm was divided into small experimental plots, each one growing a different strain of wheat. Fife was determined to find the hardiest, healthiest and most productive strain.

In 1843, Fife received some grain seeds in the mail from a friend in Scotland. His wife, Jane, was ill at the time so he could not plant the seeds right away. When he finally got around to sowing them, it was rather late in the season. Most of the other strains were growing by this time.

At first, the new wheat seemed doomed to failure. Out of all the seeds, only one sprouted. Fife was tempted to plow the single plant under and start over with another strain of wheat. But then, he noticed something unusual about the plant. It had three stalks, and seemed to grow quickly. In fact, by mid-summer, it had caught up to the others. When most of the other strains became weakened with disease, this one remained healthy and strong.

The new plant ripened earlier than the others. Then, just as it was ready to harvest, disaster nearly struck. One of the cows broke through the garden gate, trampling and eating every plant in sight. Jane spotted the cow from the kitchen window just as its tongue was about to wrap around the tender stalk of the new wheat. She ran into the yard, waving her apron high in the air, yelling at the top of her lungs! The cow wandered away and the wheat was saved.

From this single plant, Fife was able to obtain more seeds. The new wheat was especially hardy, enabling it to survive the diseases and cold temperatures that killed other strains. It required a shorter growing season, too, which meant that it could be planted later in the spring and harvested earlier in the fall. As well as producing a high yield of grain, flour from this wheat made delicious breads and pastries.

This new variety of wheat was called Red Fife. It proved to be ideal for the rugged prairies of Canada and the northern United States. The discovery of Red Fife and other hardy varieties of wheat changed the barren prairie landscape into productive farmland. Today, this region is known as the breadbasket of the nation.

Samuel Morse
1844

Encounter in Mid-Ocean

When Samuel Morse boarded a ship in France on October 1, 1832, he was a well-known portrait painter, a man at the peak of his artistic career. By the time the ship reached New York, Morse had abandoned his life's work to pursue a dream most people would call foolish.

On the second evening of the voyage, Morse and a few other passengers gathered in the dining room for a discussion. The topic turned to electricity. One man, Dr. Charles Jackson, described his experiments with electromagnets. To make an electromagnet, he said, insulated wires must be wrapped around a metal rod. When the wires are connected to a battery, the rod becomes magnetized. The more coils of wire used around the rod, the more powerful the electromagnet becomes.

The passengers listened intently to the interesting account. Then one of them asked, "If you use more wire, won't you slow the electricity? Won't it take longer for the electricity to travel?"

Dr. Jackson shook his head. "No," he answered, "electricity passes instantly over any length of wire, even if it is a mile long."

Hours later, while most passengers were fast asleep, Samuel Morse lay awake in bed, still thinking about Dr. Jackson's words. A phrase echoed continually in his mind — "Electricity passes instantly over any length of wire."

Suppose ... he wondered ... suppose a message could be sent along with the electrical current. Would the message be carried instantly too?

The possibilities astounded Morse. Throughout the night an idea, barely a seed at the start, blossomed in his mind. By morning he had reached a decision. He would give up his work in art and devote his life to finding some way of sending messages at the speed of electricity.

The task was not an easy one. Morse knew little about electricity and was not very good with equipment or machines. Progress was slow, but after three years he had made a primitive instrument that he called a telegraph. He mounted an electromagnet on a board, then hung a pendulum nearby. To the bottom of the pendulum he fastened a pencil. Then he stretched a strip of paper across the board under the pencil. By using a clock mechanism, the paper could be moved from one side of the board to the other.

To send a message, Morse controlled the flow of electricity to the coils of the electromagnet. When he switched the power on, the electromagnet was activated. It pulled the pendulum across the paper, and the pencil scribbled a mark. When he cut the power off, the electromagnet released the pendulum and etched another mark on the moving paper. By using a crude letter code, the squiggly lines could be translated into a message.

Did the telegraph work? Yes, but it was far from perfect. The power from the batteries was too weak to send the message a great distance.

To solve this problem, Morse invented the relay. He placed an electric battery along a new line to boost the power every time the circuit was closed. By using a number of relays, he found he could send messages any distance almost instantly.

By now Samuel Morse had invested six years of his life into the invention. He was penniless, his reputation as a fine artist had long been forgotten, and there was little interest in his telegraph.

Then he met Alfred Vail. This young man had the mechanical skill to help make the telegraph a more efficient device. Vail and Morse redesigned the telegraph. They removed the pendulum, pencil and zig-zag lines. Instead, they rigged the electromagnet to activate a key that printed a series of dots and dashes on paper. Using a code that Morse invented, the dots and dashes could be translated into letters of the alphabet — and then into a message.

Morse set up an experimental line between Baltimore and Washington, a distance of about

60 kilometers (40 miles). On May 24, 1844, crowds gathered at both places to watch a demonstration of the new invention.

In Washington, Morse tapped out a message: "What hath God wrought?" Instantly, Vail's telegraph in Baltimore clicked and clacked the dots and dashes on its tape, and Vail decoded the message. The crowd was interested, but unimpressed. There was nothing spectacular in the message. Some even said it was a hoax.

Then fate lent a helping hand. By chance, a political convention was being held in Baltimore. A candidate in Washington had been nominated for an important position. As soon as the news was announced, Vail telegraphed it to Morse in Washington. The candidate was standing right beside Morse! Morse translated the message. The candidate refused the offer on the spot, and Morse telegraphed the message back to Vail in Baltimore.

The demonstration was spectacular! Rather than taking the usual hours or even days to send a message, it had all been accomplished in minutes with the new telegraph. The crowd was speechless. Now they were convinced that the telegraph was a rapid, reliable way to send messages.

Soon telegraph lines sprang up all over the world, and Samuel Morse received the recognition he so richly deserved.

Mysterious Deaths

In 1846 doctors at Vienna's General Hospital in Austria were faced with a puzzling problem.

Why were so many mothers and babies in the maternity ward dying of childbed fever? And why was the death rate in one maternity ward many times higher than in another?

The hospital served many women who were charity cases. These women could not afford costly medical care. In return for medical attention for themselves and their babies, they agreed to be part of the training program for medical students. Surprisingly, the death rate in this training ward was *ten times higher* than in another ward where babies were delivered by experienced women known as midwives.

Dr. Ignaz Semmelweis was determined to unravel the mystery of these strange deaths. He observed the wards and patients closely. With the other doctors, he examined the dead bodies carefully in the hope of uncovering some clues.

Then one day there was an unfortunate accident. One of the doctors cut his finger as he dissected a dead body. Even though the cut was only a minor one, the doctor soon felt ill. He developed a fever and in a few days died of blood poisoning.

Semmelweis noticed that the doctor's

symptoms were suspiciously like those of the patients who had died of childbed fever. Acting on a hunch, he watched the movements of the doctors and students. An interesting pattern began to emerge.

Midwives who attended patients in the healthier ward did not examine bodies in the dissecting room. But doctors and students often went directly from the dissecting room to the maternity ward with the higher death rate.

All at once the pieces of the puzzle began to fit together. Semmelweis realized that the doctors and students were carrying infection from the dead bodies to the maternity ward. None of them ever stopped to wash their hands before going from one room to the other.

Semmelweis announced a new rule. From now on, patients, students and doctors had to wash and disinfect their hands. Soon, just as he suspected, the death rate dropped remarkably.

Despite the success of his methods, Ignaz Semmelweis was ridiculed by other doctors. They refused to believe that such a simple procedure could solve the problem. Semmelweis was forced to leave Vienna. His rule was forgotten and again the death rate began to climb.

Years later, doctors around the world admitted that Ignaz Semmelweis was right. Today cleanliness is recognized as one of the necessary steps in preventing the spread of disease.

John and Will Kellogg
1894

From Mush to Flakes

Like millions of other people you probably start your day with a bowl of cereal and milk. Dr. John Harvey Kellogg would be pleased!

Dr. Kellogg had firm beliefs about nutrition. He refused to consume tea, coffee, alcohol, spices and especially meat. Instead he relied on vegetarian foods — mixtures of fruits, vegetables and grains.

In the 1880s, Dr. Kellogg operated a medical boarding house in Battle Creek, Michigan. During their stay, patients were expected to follow Dr. Kellogg's prescription for health — plenty of fresh air, exercise, a good night's rest and, of course, Dr. Kellogg's diet.

Most of the patients did well at the clinic and soon got better. But the vegetarian meals were tasteless to those who enjoyed spicier meat dishes. Dr. Kellogg wanted his patients to stay on his diet even after they left the center so he began experimenting with ways to make his food taste better. He spent every evening in the hospital kitchen boiling and mashing steamed grains and vegetables. Pretty soon he was able to offer a wider choice of tasty meatless dishes on the hospital menu.

In 1894 Dr. Kellogg and his younger brother, Will Keith, began searching for an easily digested bread substitute. Boiling grains, they knew, removed starch and created new flavours and textures. So each evening the brothers boiled a pot of wheat. Next, they passed it through rollers to flatten it. They never got around to baking the flattened mixtures, though — the gooey dough always stuck in globs to the rollers. The brothers had to scrape the mess off and throw it away.

Then one evening while they were boiling yet another batch of wheat, the Kellogg brothers were unexpectedly called away on urgent business. They hurried out of the kitchen, leaving the boiled wheat to cool in the pot. By the time they got back to their experiments two days later, the overboiled mush had started to go moldy.

Instead of throwing it out, the brothers continued their experiment. To their surprise, the wheat passed smoothly through the rollers. Each grain formed a separate flake, and each flake toasted evenly in the oven! Why? By leaving the wheat to sit, moisture had seeped evenly into each kernel.

With more experimenting, the Kelloggs found the perfect formula for boiling and sitting that produced light, tasty — and unmoldy — wheat flakes. By using a similar method, they went on to make rice, corn and bran flakes too.

Dr. Kellogg was satisfied with the flakes purely from a health point of view. Not so with

Will. He saw the business opportunities. Eventually he bought his brother's share of the flake invention, processed and packaged the flake cereal in Battle Creek and created a breakfast food empire.

Clarence Birdseye
About 1917

Fresh Frozen

It seemed that Clarence Birdseye had always been interested in two things — food and animals. He had even taken cooking classes in high school to learn more about animals and ways to prepare food. But unusual circumstances — not school lessons — helped Clarence Birdseye with his most famous food discovery.

Between 1914 and 1917, Clarence lived as a fur trader in Labrador. Fresh food was not always available in the sub-zero climate, but Birdseye noticed that the native peoples rarely went hungry. Why not? After a fishing or hunting expedition, they stored part of their catch outdoors. In the cold, dry air the food froze quickly. Months later, as the need arose, they would thaw and cook their frozen food.

Probably hundreds of fur traders had noticed this unusual way of preserving food, but Clarence Birdseye was the first one to think about the possibilities. He found that meat frozen on the coldest days tasted fresher and more tender than meat frozen at other times. He examined the meat under his microscope to find out why. The meat that froze more slowly formed long thin ice needles inside that punctured the cell walls. As the meat thawed, the broken cell walls collapsed, fluid seeped out and the food tasted bland and soggy. But the meat that was frozen quickly on very cold days didn't have time to form the damaging needle-like crystals. Its cell walls remained unbroken, and the food was firm and tasty.

Birdseye tested his findings with other types of food. He soaked a few cabbages in salt water and then set them outside in the freezing wind. The cabbages quickly froze, their cells unbroken by ice crystals.

Now that he knew how freezing preserved foods, Birdseye was ready to tackle another problem. Somehow he had to find a convenient way to quickly freeze food in warmer climates.

When he returned to the United States in 1923, he experimented with rabbit meat and fresh fillets in his own kitchen. Later he worked in a refrigeration plant in New Jersey. Eventually he invented a freezing machine. In it, very cold salt water was passed over metal plates that touched the cartons of food. Food could be frozen in minutes instead of hours!

By the end of the 1920s, Birdseye began selling packages of his frozen foods. People soon discovered that the quick-frozen food tasted as fresh as the day it was frozen.

The frozen food business made Clarence Birdseye a wealthy man. His success must have given him the urge to invent, too, for by the time he died in 1956, at the age of seventy-three, he had over 300 other inventions to his credit.

Christian K. Nelson
1920

Two Tastes in One Bite

It took a young boy with a difficult decision to give Christian Nelson his bright idea.

Nelson owned an ice cream and candy store in Onowa, Iowa. One day a boy came into the store, clutching a few coins in his hand. At first he asked for a chocolate bar. Just as Nelson reached for one, the boy changed his mind. No, he decided, make that an ice cream sandwich. Nelson began to cut a slice of ice cream, preparing to put it between two wafers. Again the boy changed his mind. No, he wanted the chocolate bar after all. He chose one, laid his precious money on the counter and left.

The incident stuck with Christian Nelson for some time. It seemed that neither the chocolate bar nor the ice cream sandwich could make the boy *entirely* happy. Why couldn't he have both? Why not freeze a chocolate coating around a slice of ice cream?

Using every spare minute he could find, Christian Nelson experimented with mixtures of chocolate and ice cream in a back room of his store. The idea was simple enough — but *doing* it was tricky. No matter what Nelson tried, the chocolate wouldn't stick to the ice cream.

One day he mentioned his problem to a candy salesman. Chocolate candy manufacturers, the salesman explained, use cocoa butter to make the chocolate stick to the candy centres.

So Nelson tried again. This time he changed the quantities of cocoa butter. Late one night he dipped a slice of ice cream into a heated chocolate mixture, and the chocolate coating solidified onto the ice cream, at last!

The chocolate ice cream bar was a great success, and Christian Nelson became a wealthy man. Now it was possible for indecisive people, like the little boy who had visited his shop, to satisfy two cravings with one bite!

Experimental Twists

Think of the words "scientist" ... "inventor" ... What comes to mind?

It's likely that you get an image of an odd-looking man in a cluttered laboratory surrounded by dozens of bubbling mixtures. The man is tinkering with bottles, vials and test tubes. As he pours one solution into another, the liquid froths and changes color. Clouds of choking smoke billow across the room. Clearly something has gone wrong.

This is the image often painted of scientists and inventors. It is a distorted image, but in one way, at least, it is accurate.

Experiments do not always go as planned. Sometimes the results are unusual, unexpected, even disappointing.

These surprises aren't necessarily *bad*. Sometimes unforeseen kinks in an experiment can force a scientist or inventor to pause, study the situation and see possibilities he has never even dreamed of before. Sometimes a twist of fate during an experiment can be the key that unlocks the door to a totally new discovery.

Joseph Priestly
1774

Sudden Brightness

Young Joseph Priestly could only watch other children play games and sports. He was a pale, sickly child, too frail to join in most activities. So instead of training his body, Joseph trained his mind. He read books, learned other languages and spent hours observing nature. Years later these childhood interests would lead him, almost by accident, to one of the most important discoveries of the eighteenth century.

As a child Joseph Priestly collected insects. He was fascinated by how they lived. Often he put them in sealed bottles to see how long they could survive in the same air. Young Joseph wasn't being willfully cruel. He conducted these experiments because he was intrigued with gases and how living things used them.

When he was older, Joseph Priestly became a church minister. He set up a laboratory in his home and continued his experiments with gases. He invented a device for collecting gases over a surface of water. At another time, he combined air and water to produce a tingly, gassy, pleasant-tasting mixture. His "soda water" became a popular drink, and a delighted Priestly whipped up batches for his friends.

But Priestly was still mainly interested in how air supported life. He refined the insect experiments that he had conducted as a child. One experiment involved filling a jar with "common" or ordinary air and observing how long a mouse could survive in the jar. When Priestly collected air from stagnant pools nearby and repeated the experiment, he found that a mouse could not live as long in this air. He concluded that there must be different kinds of air, with different properties.

In 1774, at the age of forty-one, Priestly began to use chemicals to manufacture different gases. By focusing the sun's rays through a magnifying glass, he was able to burn mercuric oxide, a reddish powder. He collected the gas that was released and stored it in bottles.

Priestly spent many hours collecting and storing gas and might have continued this way for some time if it hadn't been for an unexpected flash of insight. During one of his gas-collecting experiments with mercuric oxide, he happened to have a lighted candle nearby. Suddenly a thought crossed his mind, a twist on his insect and mouse experiments. Why not use the *candle* in the jar?

He grabbed the candle and thrust it into the jar. The flame grew in size, flaring vigorously and burning even brighter than before. What a surprise!

Priestly quickly devised other tests for this strange gas. He took a glowing stick from the fireplace and lowered it into another jar of the gas. Instantly it burst into flames. Then Priestly repeated his mouse experiment. In a jar of ordinary air a mouse could survive only fifteen minutes. In this gas, it could live *twice as long*. Finally he conducted a test on himself. Cautiously he took a whiff of the gas and felt a lightness in his chest after inhaling it.

Priestly's experiments proved that this gas improved both breathing and burning, but he missed the true value of his discovery. Later, a French scientist, Antoine Lavoisier, proved that the gas produced by heating mercuric oxide was not air at all, but a new chemical element. He named the gas oxygen. Today we know that oxygen, one of several gases in air, is necessary for both burning and breathing.

The unexpected, brilliant glow of a candle has changed our lives more than Joseph Priestly could have imagined. Today, we use oxygen in industry to produce higher temperatures for burning and welding. In hospitals, oxygen aids patients who have difficulty breathing.

But there have been even more astounding changes. By producing oxygen and taking it with him, man has been able to visit areas where there isn't any air. Every day there are breakthroughs in space research and in underwater and underground exploration. Joseph Priestly's candle began a series of discoveries that continues even today.

Louis Daguerre
1835

Pictures Without Painting

Today you can take a photograph with a camera and have it developed in just a few minutes. It wasn't always this way.

In the early 1800s, the only way to produce an image was by painting it. Louis Daguerre, a French artist and stage designer, created landscapes and nature backdrops that were strikingly realistic. But Daguerre was not satisfied. Surely, he thought, there must be some way to make pictures directly, some method of capturing images without having to use paint and canvas.

Louis Daguerre was so obsessed with this dream that he spent twenty years searching for this magical process. He conducted experiment after experiment with chemicals, metals and camera-like devices. All his attempts failed.

Then, luckily, Daguerre heard of another French inventor, Niecephore Niepce, who had some — but not much — success with "fixing" an image permanently on a light sensitive surface. The two men formed a partnership and shared information. When Niepce died in 1833, Daguerre continued his experiments alone.

Quite by accident, Daguerre finally hit upon the process for producing images. One day after treating a metal sheet with iodine, he carelessly laid a silver spoon on its surface. When he removed the spoon later, he noticed an odd thing — a faint image of it remained on the metal!

Using this accident as a clue, Daguerre treated a polished silver plate with iodine. thereby forming a thin layer of silver iodide. When he exposed the iodized plate to light, a hazy picture appeared on it. There were two problems, though. The picture required a long exposure time, and it soon faded because Daguerre didn't know how to fix it permanently on the plate.

Nevertheless, he continued his experiments with light-sensitive silver plates. One spring day in 1835, he felt tired earlier than usual. He had just exposed a silver plate to light, but for only a short time. No image had yet appeared. Before going to bed, Daguerre stored the under-exposed plate in his chemical cupboard.

The next morning, when he went to the cupboard to get the plate, he couldn't believe his eyes. Perhaps he was still asleep, he thought, for on the plate was a picture. Somehow, over-night, a picture had fully developed — on its own!

Daguerre knew that he was close to an important discovery. He suspected something in the cupboard must have developed the image. If he could find that substance, he could drastically shorten the exposure time for the picture.

Each day Daguerre deliberately put under-exposed plates in the cupboard. Each day he removed one more chemical from the shelves. Still the plates mysteriously continued to develop.

Finally, when there were no more chemicals left in the cupboard, Daguerre again stored a plate in it. By morning, an image had appeared on the plate. Daguerre was mystified. At last he spotted a few drops of spilled mercury in the corner of the cupboard. Mercury vapor! Daguerre realized that the vapor must have made the images develop.

By using mercury vapor, Daguerre could shorten the exposure time. One problem still remained. Over time the images darkened. Luckily, after a few more years of experimenting, Louis Daguerre discovered that another chemical, sodium hyposulfate, could "fix" the image on a plate. Now an image could be exposed on a light-sensitive surface, developed and then fixed permanently, never to fade again.

On August 10, 1839, the French Academy of Fine Arts and the French Academy of Sciences together honoured Niepce and Daguerre, the two men who had discovered how to print images on silver.

Daguerre was triumphant. His perseverance was finally rewarded. Perhaps, though, he may have paused to ponder the role that fate, a silver spoon and a few spilled drops of mercury had played in his great discovery.

A Blast of Cold Air

On the day in 1855 that fate changed Henry Bessemer's life, he was busy as usual in his iron-works factory in London, England. The air inside was hot and humid. Drops of moisture trickled down the inventor's face as he paced nervously in front of a fiery furnace. Then, unable to wait any longer, Bessemer issued an order to the workmen around him.

"Open the door," he shouted. "Let's take a look!"

Scorching heat poured from the furnace as the door swung open. Shielding his eyes from the brilliant glow, Bessemer used a long rod to poke the iron bars inside. Sparks showered upward with each stab of the rod. The bars were still solid! Bessemer was disappointed. What could be wrong?

Henry Bessemer was already a successful inventor. He had created a special type of gold paint, a new kind of pencil and an interesting method of stamping official documents. In 1854 he had designed a revolutionary new cannon shell, one that rotated or turned as it whistled through the air. This new shell could cover greater distances than ordinary cannon shot. But the task facing Bessemer in his ironworks factory was the most challenging yet.

Bessemer had been trying to produce steel for some time. Steel was a highly prized metal, a special combination of iron and carbon. Steel was tougher than iron, yet it could be hammered or rolled into sheets while it was still hot.

Steel was also tricky to produce. Iron bars had to be melted in the searing heat of a charcoal fire. In the process, the molten iron absorbed carbon from the burning charcoal. If just the right amount of carbon was absorbed, the metal became steel. If too much carbon was absorbed, the metal became hard, brittle and unbendable.

Bessemer was puzzled by the solid bars before him. Obviously the fire was not hot enough, but if he burned *more* charcoal he would be adding too much carbon to the iron. He dared not add more. In desperation he ordered the fire bridge of the furnace opened. This would let in a blast of cold air to fan the fire.

A half-hour crept past. Again Bessemer ordered the door opened. Inside the bars glowed white hot. They looked unchanged. Using the metal rod, Bessemer nudged a bar deeper into the furnace and it crumbled! Liquid iron oozed out from it. Surprisingly, the bars had looked solid, but only a thin shell had covered the melted insides.

Bessemer was stunned. Enormous quantities of charcoal had failed to melt the iron, but a simple blast of cold air had succeeded. Why?

Excitedly, he reviewed the facts. Burning was a chemical reaction. Carbon in the fuel combined with oxygen in the air to release great heat. By opening the fire bridge, Bessemer had added oxygen. To produce the extra heat, carbon must have been added too. Yet he *hadn't* added more fuel. What was the mysterious source of carbon?

Then it hit him. Of course. The iron itself! The carbon in the iron had combined with the oxygen to produce such an intense heat that the iron had melted.

Bessemer was thrilled by the possibilities of his find. Here was a way to produce the high temperatures he needed while at the same time ridding the iron of the carbon that made it brittle. If he could control how much carbon was burned off, he could also control the quality of metal he made. He was close to the secret of producing strong, flexible steel.

Bessemer designed a converter, a container where crude iron could be changed into steel. He constructed a simple cylinder about four feet high. A hole in the flat top became the escape hatch. By adding tiny holes and pipes in the bottom, air blown into the converter could be controlled.

During the first test, compressed air was blown upward through the molten iron. Bessemer and his workers waited eagerly to see what would happen. Suddenly, like a volcanic eruption, sparks and flames spewed from the escape hatch. Molten metal splashed high into the air. Everyone ran for cover.

After twenty minutes the flames died down and the men gathered around the converter. Bessemer ladled the white-hot metal into a mold. When he tested it, he found that the metal was strong, yet he could hammer or roll without cracking or breaking it. It was exactly the type of metal Bessemer wanted.

Bessemer improved his converter, tipping it at an angle to prevent liquid iron from shooting out. Then he took out a patent for his method of steel production.

In 1858 Bessemer established his own steel company. In a short time the firm of Henry Bessemer and Company was turning out large quantities of high quality steel at one-fifth its former price. Gradually, in the face of such competition, other ironworkers began manufacturing steel using Bessemer's method.

With a cheap source of strong, flexible steel, the construction industry boomed. Steel produced Bessemer's way was used in ships, skyscrapers, railyards, bridges and machinery. A quick blast of air had unexpectedly triggered the start of the modern steel age!

Miracle Box

A simple suggestion from a friend changed George Eastman's life. It also changed the way we take pictures.

From the time he was a teenager, George Eastman had worked long hard hours at a New York bank to support his widowed mother and two sisters. In 1874, at the age of twenty-four, he was finally able to afford his first vacation. He planned a trip abroad.

"George," his friend said, "why don't you buy a camera? Then you could have pictures of your trip to show us."

George Eastman thought this was a dandy idea! He rushed out and bought his first camera. It was an expensive, heavy device that was almost as big as an apple crate. To use it he needed other expensive gear — a heavy tripod, bulky photographic glass plates, a dark tent inside which he would spread a sticky light-sensitive jelly on the plates before exposure, chemicals, glass tanks and other items to develop the pictures. Instructions for the proper use of these materials cost another five dollars.

George Eastman soon realized that taking pictures on his trip would be no easy task. Clearly a less expensive and simpler system was needed.

An idea began to take shape in George

Eastman's mind. He immediately cancelled his trip and concentrated on improving the complicated picture-taking process. His first task was to find a substitute for the messy wet jelly that had to be smeared on the glass plates in darkness.

Months of trial and error followed. Each evening, after a full day at the bank, Eastman mixed and cooked emulsions in his mother's kitchen. Often he worked late into the night until he finally collapsed, falling asleep on a blanket by the kitchen stove.

After numerous frustrations and several unsuitable products, Eastman came up with a convenient mix. A layer of light-sensitive flexible celluloid could be fastened to a paper backing. No more heavy glass plates!

Unfortunately, only a few professional photographers tried out the new film. Most people still shied away from the bulky, expensive camera and accessories. But George Eastman would not give up. He was determined to put photography into everybody's hands.

Eventually he developed a simple black box-type camera that anyone could use. The light, flexible film was wound on a spool at the back of the box. To take a picture all you had to do was aim the camera and press a button to release the shutter. By turning a key outside the box, you advanced the film to the next frame, ready to take another picture. No more tents, messy chemicals or heavy equipment to lug around!

In June 1888, the first of Eastman's cameras went on sale. Fully loaded and ready to use, each sold for twenty-five dollars. Eastman named his new cameras Kodaks. The name was simple, easy to spell and easy to remember.

At first, when you wanted to develop your pictures, you had to send the whole camera, with the film still inside, to Rochester, New York, for processing. The photographs and your newly-loaded camera were then returned to you. Of course, that meant you couldn't take any pictures until your camera came back. Later, with more improvements, professional photographers in each city were able to develop the film. Now you could keep your camera with you, and buy and load new film whenever you wished.

Kodaks were a great success around the world, and George Eastman became enormously wealthy.

When Eastman died in 1932, the heavy, awkward type of camera that he had purchased for the holiday he never took, had disappeared. A simple, small, light box — much like the one you probably use today — had taken its place. George Eastman got his wish — the miracle of photography was now available to everyone.

Alexander Graham Bell
1875

Faint Musical Tones

For months two men had steadily worked at the tangle of wire, springs, reeds and electromagnets in their attic laboratory. Yet Alexander Graham Bell, an inventor and teacher of the deaf, and his assistant, Thomas Watson, were no closer to their goal than when they had started.

Bell and Watson were striving to improve the telegraph. In the early 1870s, the telegraph was the most efficient and fastest way to send a message over a long distance. Let's say you wanted to send a message to a friend who lived very far away. At your end, an operator would read your message, then use a code of clicks and clacks to tap out each letter on the telegraph key. Every time the key was held down, a surge of electricity would shoot along a wire to a receiver in your friend's town. There, another telegraph machine would tap out the same click or clack sounds that had been transmitted. Another operator would decode the message, write it down and deliver it to your friend.

Unfortunately, only a single message could be sent along a telegraph wire at any one time. Bell and Watson had been struggling to find some way to send several messages at once along a single wire.

On the afternoon of June 2, 1875, the situation seemed completely hopeless.

At one end of the attic where they worked, Watson tapped the keys of his telegraph transmitter. Across the attic, in another room, Bell pressed his ear to the receiver, tuning each reed one by one. Suddenly there was an accident.

One of Watson's transmitter springs jammed. He snapped at the spring, trying to set it free. Again and again he plucked the spring.

In the other room, Bell bent low, listening to the reeds as he adjusted them. All at once he heard a faint musical hum from one of his receiver reeds.

Bell raced from the room shouting, "What did you do then? Don't touch anything! Let me see!"

Thomas Watson showed him that the spring on the transmitter had stuck and how he had tried to pluck it loose. Bell ordered him to keep plucking while he returned to his room and pressed his ear against the receiver.

Again Bell heard the hum. To his sensitive ear, the sound was exactly the same pitch and loudness as Watson's plucked spring.

This mishap showed Bell that a sound could be sent over wire and duplicated exactly in a receiver. Over the next months, Bell and Watson worked at improving their device.

Finally on the morning of Friday, March 10, 1876, Bell spoke into a mouthpiece. At the other end of the line, several rooms away, Watson heard the muffled message in his receiver: "Mr. Watson, come here. I want you!" Thomas Watson rushed to Bell and repeated his message.

Instead of a cumbersome series of clicks and clacks, the two men had succeeded in transmitting far more — the human voice! With hard work, a lucky chance and careful observation, one of our modern marvels, the telephone, had come of age.

Elihu Thomson
1876

Flash of Green

No other science class could quite match Elihu Thomson's. While most teachers in the 1870s taught only by lecturing, Thomson's classes were filled with lively, dynamic demonstrations. He challenged his students at Central High School in Philadelphia to think, question and then experiment in the school laboratory, the only one of its kind in the United States.

As the young professor's popularity grew, he was often asked to be a speaker at public functions. In the fall of 1876, the Franklin Institute, a group of distinguished scientists, invited him to give five winter lectures to its members.

Following his usual style, Thomson carefully prepared his material and included several demonstrations to highlight key points. The first four lectures went as planned. The fifth did not.

In the last lecture, Thomson wanted to show electricity in action. On a table in front of his audience he had placed a Leyden jar, an insulated bottle that could store electricity.

Beside it, he had a hand-operated electrostatic generator and several copper wires.

First, Thomson connected the electrostatic machine to the Leyden jar. He cranked it vigorously, sending electric charges to the jar, where they were stored. In this way, he would have a large source of electricity ready for use.

He planned to cross two copper wires that led away from the Leyden jar. A sudden spark would show that electricity had passed from one wire to another.

The audience knew of Thomson's reputation for showmanship. No one wanted to miss the action. The hall was hushed, all eyes riveted on the equipment at the front.

Thomson carefully brought the wires together. But instead of a spark, there was a bright green flash. Thompson was startled. He picked up the two wires. They were solidly welded together!

Although Thomson knew that something special had happened, he did not want to lose his audience. He dismissed the unusual incident with a casual remark and continued his lecture.

Later in his laboratory, Thompson toyed with the fused wires. The unexpected welding interested him. He was certain that he was on the brink of an important discovery.

Elihu Thomson couldn't experiment with electric welding right away, though. Eight long years would pass before the development of a source of electricity strong enough to melt metals and fuse them together.

Once this hurdle was passed, the advantages to electric welding became obvious. Dozens of industries from shipbuilding to toy manufacturing were able to use welding to cleanly and simply join metal parts.

Elihu Thomson was more than a skilled teacher. He was a man of vision who could see grand possibilities in a strange green flash of light.

Louis Pasteur
1880

A Weakened Strain of Bacteria

Smallpox, scarlet fever, polio! Years ago these were common diseases. Today early vaccinations have made them almost non-existent. It took a bit of carelessness over one hundred years ago to lead a brilliant scientist to this discovery.

Louis Pasteur, a chemistry professor in Paris, believed that microscopic organisms, caused diseases. Germs were outside the body, he said, and diseases started when the germs entered the body. Not many people shared his belief, but Pasteur was determined to show the world that he was right.

Around 1880, he began to study a contagious animal disease known as chicken cholera. An associate sent him the head of a rooster that had died of the disease. Convinced that the rooster's blood contained the germs that had caused the disease, Pasteur decided to isolate them.

First he prepared a bottle of broth from chicken gristle. He added a drop of the rooster's blood and placed the liquid in a warm place. With food and warmth, the germs multiplied rapidly. After a few hours Pasteur checked a drop of the broth under his microscope. He could see hundreds of germs swarming in the culture!

Pasteur tried an experiment. He mixed a tiny drop of the culture with a chicken's food. Soon after eating the mixture, the chicken was dead.

Pasteur tested the effects again and again. Each time a chicken died. As he had suspected, disease could be transmitted by germs from one animal to another.

Fascinated by his experiments, Pasteur worked long and hard. Finally, concerned with his health, his wife convinced him to go on a well deserved vacation with his family. He left his two assistants to look after the cholera cultures.

In his absence, his overworked assistants decided that they needed a holiday too. For weeks the cultures were left unattended. Many of the germs died and the strain weakened.

When he returned, Pasteur was furious, but he was also intrigued by new possibilities.

He injected several chickens with the weakened cultures. Instead of dying as before, the chickens became only slightly ill, then completely recovered. This was new!

Pasteur began an experiment with two groups of chickens. One, the control group, had never had injections of cholera. The second group had already been given injections of weakened cholera germs. Now Pasteur injected all the chickens with a fresh cholera culture. Then he waited.

Over the space of a few hours, the chickens

in the control group died one by one. The chickens in the second group remained healthy! Injecting an animal with weak or dead germs seemed to cause a slight case of the disease, just enough to provide protection if the animal contracted a fatal dose of the disease.

At first Pasteur believed he could control all kinds of infectious diseases with injections of stale cholera germs. He soon discovered that cholera vaccinations provided protection only against cholera. Other diseases were caused by specialized germs and had to be treated with cultures of those specific germs.

Louis Pasteur's work with neglected and weakened cultures has resulted in the development of vaccines that protect millions of people around the world from diseases that a hundred years ago would have caused countless deaths.

Thomas L. Willson
1892

Surprising Bubbles

Thomas L. Willson was a creative genius with a flair for recognizing opportunities that others missed. It's not surprising that he could discover one thing while looking for another.

Willson showed an interest in science at an early age. While other children played games or indulged in pranks, young Willson puttered in the makeshift laboratory he had built in the cellar of his parent's home in Hamilton, Ontario.

His laboratory was a clutter of odds and ends. Willson saved everything. Discarded wooden crates and planks became furniture. Bottles, jars, string, wire, metal, rocks — even dismantled kitchen gadgets — all became equipment for his projects.

Willson's talent soon became obvious. By the time he was fifteen, he had already built a dynamo, a machine which generates electricity. His was one of the first dynamos in Canada. By nineteen, he had also invented a powerful electric light called an arc lamp. He hooked it up to the dynamo and hung it outside. People gathered from near and far to catch a glimpse of this sensational new invention.

Willson soon became interested in the arc furnace, a device which produces high temperatures using electricity. By this time though, he was rather short of money, and accepted a job with a chemical company. Once again, he displayed his talent for spotting the unexpected.

In the 1890s, many chemical companies were interested in aluminum, a light-weight metal with many valuable properties. Unlike other metals, such as gold and silver, aluminum could not be found in the earth in its pure form. It was locked in aluminum compounds such as aluminum chloride. Extracting the aluminum was a complicated and expensive process.

Two separate reactions were commonly used to free the aluminum from its compound. First, sodium was produced by heating lime, soda and powdered iron at high temperatures in the arc furnace. Then, the sodium reacted with aluminum chloride to release the aluminum from the compound.

Willson knew that the process could be made less expensive if another metal were used instead of sodium. Believing that calcium might be a good substitute, he concentrated his time and energies on finding a cheap and plentiful supply of it.

Willson experimented unsuccessfully with many mixtures. One day in 1892, he tried something different. He mixed lime and coal tar in a container, popped it into the arc furnace and raised the temperature to 2800 C. Then he waited.

When enough time had passed, Willson

carefully opened the furnace door and removed the container. The mixture looked different! It had become hard, brittle and crystalline. What was it — calcium, sodium or some other substance?

Willson knew that even a tiny chunk of sodium would spin wildly in a container of water, producing hydrogen gas in the process. He decided to try a simple test. He broke off a small piece of the unknown substance and cautiously dropped it into a bucket of water.

The material foamed slowly and quietly. Clearly, this was not sodium. Suddenly, Willson's attention was drawn to the bubbles that popped quietly on the surface of the water. What gas was being produced? Was it hydrogen?

In fact, the crystalline substance that formed in the arc furnace turned out to be what Willson had hoped — a calcium compound called calcium carbide. Using Willson's method, this chemical could be produced cheaply in unlimited quantities. It's price at the time dropped from $10,000 a pound ($22,000 a kilo) to 1 cent a pound (2.2 cents a kilo)! Thomas Willson earned the nickname "Carbide Willson" for his achievement.

But Willson's second discovery was perhaps even more important. The unknown gas was identified as acetylene. Willson had found a simple way to produce it — just allow calcium carbide to react with water! Because he had found an abundant source of calcium carbide, acetylene could be made economically, in large quantities.

Within the next few years, many uses were found for acetylene, from the production of fertilizers to the manufacturing of automobile headlights. In 1903, with the invention of the oxyacetylene torch, a way to harness the intense heat of burning acetylene was found. With the narrow flame of the oxyacetylene torch, thick metal plates could be sliced apart or easily fused and welded together.

During his lifetime, Thomas Willson collected over 70 patents for his inventions and breakthroughs. But perhaps his greatest achievement was the unexpected discovery of acetylene from calcium carbide.

Wilhelm Rontgen
1895

Glow in the Dark

On the evening of November 8, 1895, Wilhelm Rontgen hurried through an experiment so he could get home in time for dinner. In his rush he made an error, stumbled across a great scientific discovery, missed dinner, and stepped into the pages of history.

Rontgen had been working with a long glass tube called a cathode ray tube. It had a metal plate at each end, and was empty. When these plates were hooked up to the terminals of a battery, a type of radiation known as cathode rays was produced inside the tube.

Cathode rays caused the glass walls of the tube to fluoresce or to glow an eerie lime-green color. Because these rays could penetrate a few inches of air, the air directly around the tube, and even special chemicals held close to the tube, became fluorescent as well. But cathode rays had no effect on materials that were farther away.

In his experiment, Rontgen had wrapped the tube completely with a sheet of heavy black paper. He planned to set up a chemically treated cardboard screen just inches from the tube. If his hunch was correct, cathode rays would be able to go through the paper, and make the screen glow!

Rontgen shut off the lights in his room and turned on the cathode ray tube. No light was visible. He looked towards the screen to see if it was fluorescent, but it wasn't in place. In his rush, Rontgen had forgotten to set it up!

Rontgen glanced around the black room to where he thought he had left the screen.

His eyes opened wide in amazement. A ghostly green light shimmered from across the room.

Rontgen quickly shut off the current to the cathode ray tube. The green glow vanished. He turned the current back on — and the green glow returned. Finally he struck a match to see where the glow originated. It was the cardboard screen he had left lying on a bench across the room!

Rontgen knew cathode rays couldn't travel that far. The tube had to be giving off *another* type of radiation.

Throughout the night and during the following day, he performed many experiments with the invisible mystery ray. Rontgen knew that the ray could travel through air, but would it travel through other objects too? It did! Paper, glass, wood, rubber and other materials could not block the ray. It travelled through them as if they weren't even there. Only one substance, lead, seemed to stop the ray.

But the most surprising property of the ray was discovered by chance. One day while he had the cathode ray tube switched on, Rontgen moved a small piece of lead in its path. Behind it, on a screen, he saw the shadow of the metal as he had expected, but with it a startling sight — an outline of the bones in his own hand! The rays could penetrate human flesh!

Rontgen asked his wife to help in his next experiment. She held her hand between the cathode ray tube and an unexposed photographic plate. When the plate was developed, Rontgen was delighted. He saw a permanent picture of the bones of his wife's hand surrounded by a dim outline of the flesh. His wife, however, was not so pleased. Convinced that she had seen the ghost of her own hand, she refused to participate in any more experiments with the strange ray!

Because so much was unknown about these rays, Rontgen called them X-rays, a name we still use. Today Wilhelm Rontgen's mysterious ray has many uses, from detecting flaws in the welded joints of spaceships to enabling doctors to "see" into the human body to look for broken bones.

Mysterious Images

Henri Becquerel, a French scientist, was excited by the possibilities of his experiment. He wrapped an unexposed photographic plate in black paper and set it out in the bright sunlight. On top of the paper he placed a crystal of a uranium salt. The crystal began to glow with an unusual bluish color.

Becquerel knew that sunlight could not expose the photographic plate because it was protected by the black paper. He thought the sunlight made the crystal fluoresce or glow. If anything appeared on the plate, as he suspected it would, it had to come from the glowing crystal. That would mean that some invisible rays had been produced, rays that could pass through the paper.

When Becquerel developed the plate, he found a well-defined image of the crystal. As he expected, the glowing crystal gave off invisible rays.

On February 26, 1896, Becquerel repeated his experiment. But that day and the next two days, were so cloudy that the crystal hardly glowed at all. Becquerel decided not to wait any longer. He developed the plate, expecting to find only a faint image of the crystal.

Not so. He was surprised to find that the crystal's image was as clear as before. Amazing!

Sunlight did not seem to have any effect on the amount of rays the crystal gave off.

Quickly Becquerel set up another experiment. This time, he placed the wrapped photographic plate and the crystal inside a dark cupboard.

Surely, he thought, without any light the crystal could not fluoresce at all.

When he developed the plate a few days later, he couldn't believe his eyes. A clear impression of the crystal showed again! Even without sunlight, without glowing, the crystal still gave off rays.

There was only one explanation. The crystal must be giving off a constant stream of naturally produced, invisible rays or radiation. Becquerel had proved that some materials are "radioactive."

Several years passed before the importance of Becquerel's discovery was fully known. His work opened up a whole new branch of science, the study of the energy locked inside radioactive substances. Because of one man's curiosity and because the sun didn't shine brightly on the last few days of February 1896, the world had slipped into the nuclear age.

Alexander Fleming
1928

Clear Rings, Shrinking Patches

If someone hadn't mistakenly left a window open in Dr. Alexander Fleming's laboratory, our whole world might be very different.

In 1928, Dr. Fleming worked in a crowded laboratory in a London hospital. All around the room were dozens of small round plates called culture dishes. Each of the dishes contained patches of bacteria that Dr. Fleming had grown for study.

In September Dr. Fleming returned to his laboratory after a holiday. He was disappointed to learn that someone had accidentally left a window open overnight. Foreign bacteria had entered the culture dishes. They were contaminated. All the doctor's work was ruined.

Reluctantly, Dr. Fleming began to throw the dishes in the garbage. By chance, an assistant walked into the room and Dr. Fleming paused to show him a contaminated plate. Suddenly he stopped and looked closer. There was something odd about the dish that he hadn't noticed before.

A mold like one you might find on bread or cheese was growing at the top edge of the plate. Around the mold, in a ring, was a clear space where bacteria were not growing. Fleming noticed that some of the patches of bacteria near that clear ring were shrivelling or dissolving.

Fascinated by this unusual find, Dr. Fleming took a speck of mold off the dish and put it in some broth where it could grow. Several days later he began experimenting with the broth. When he added a few drops of the broth to other culture plates, he found that some of the bacteria were destroyed while others remained unaffected. When he injected some of the broth into a rabbit, the rabbit stayed healthy. It seemed safe to use. Fleming also compared his mold with other kinds of mold. None of them had the same effect on bacteria as *his* broth.

After years of research, Dr. Fleming was able to extract a drug from the special mold. The new drug could control the growth of some kinds of bacteria. Dr. Fleming called it penicillin because it came from the penicillium mold. Today penicillin is one of the most commonly used and effective antibiotics available.

Some time later Dr. Fleming acknowledged the role of chance in his discovery. "I have been wonderfully lucky," he said. Luck certainly did play a part in the discovery of penicillin, but Dr. Fleming deserves credit, too. Without his keen observations and years of patient research, the opportunity that fate provided would have been missed or thrown away.

Surprise Endings

Two hundred years ago, John Spilsbury, a British teacher, tried out a new learning aid in his classroom. Today the same invention is a popular pastime around the world, something quite different than Spilsbury expected.

Many of John Spilsbury's students had difficulty remembering names and places on maps. So he invented a device to help them. He glued a map of England and Wales onto a thin piece of wood. Then he cut the wood along county boundaries. By reassembling the pieces, his students learned geography quickly.

Spilsbury thought his invention would only be used in the classroom, but others saw possibilities he didn't. Colorful pictures were substituted for the maps. These were glued onto wafers of wood, then cut into odd shaped pieces. People had fun fitting the pieces together to make up the complete picture. From John Spilsbury's educational invention came the jigsaw puzzle we still enjoy today.

As the stories in this chapter show, an inventor or scientist sometimes has one idea in mind — but then fate steps in to twist and change it. In the end a different product or plan develops. Sometimes it's even better than the original!

Levi Strauss
1848

Pants, Not Tents!

In 1848 young Levi Strauss left Bavaria and went to the United States, where he joined his older brothers peddling cloth and household goods in small towns. Then Levi heard of the California gold rush.

Like thousands of others, the idea of a fortune ready for the taking appealed to the young man. In 1849 he packed up his wares, boarded a clipper ship in New York and headed for California by way of Cape Horn in South America. Throughout the lengthy voyage, Levi peddled his goods to fellow passengers. By the time the ship reached San Francisco, he had a pocketful of money and a few rolls of canvas left unsold.

The canvas was a disappointment to Levi. He had expected to sell the cloth for use as tents and wagon covers. But no one wanted the canvas — they already had tents. "Pants. You should have brought pants!" people told him. Prospecting, Levi found out, was demanding work. Pants wore out quickly and had to be replaced often.

Levi hired a tailor to fashion pants out of his leftover canvas. They sold in a flash! Almost overnight other prospectors heard of Levi's durable trousers and wanted "Levi's" too.

Levi soon realized that the mines and rivers of California didn't house all the gold. He could have his own private gold rush! He opened a small pants manufacturing shop in San Francisco and began mass producing canvas pants.

A keen businessman, Levi looked for ways to improve his product. He switched from canvas to denim, a softer yet stronger material. To ensure that each piece of cloth would match the next, he dyed the denim indigo blue. Later he added copper rivets to strengthen the pockets.

People started calling the pants "blue denims," then eventually "blue jeans," slang for Genoa, a town in Italy where a denim-like material was made.

Today, millions of people around the globe wear jeans, the pants that started as canvas tenting in the days of the California Gold Rush.

George Crum
1853

A Chef's Revenge

Revenge was all George Crum really wanted. Unexpectedly, he produced a tasty new snack instead.

One day in 1853, this proud chef was faced with a dissatisfied customer in the restaurant of Moon Lake Lodge, a resort in Saratoga Springs, New York. The unhappy guest sent his order of french fries back to the kitchen.

"Make them thinner, saltier and crispier," the guest commanded.

George Crum steamed at the complaint. After all, he had made delicious french fries hundreds of times before. Reluctantly, he tried again. But the second batch was returned too.

Not one to give up, George whipped up a new batch of thinner, well fried slices. Once again, the hard-to-please customer rejected them.

In a huff, the frazzled chef seized a potato and cut it into slices so thin you could see through them. He soaked the slices in ice-cold water, then fried them crispy brown and salted them heavily.

With a great deal of show, he marched into the dining room and set the paper thin slices before the startled guest. George Crum was satisfied that revenge was his at last. The customer was sure to hate these overdone, oversalted potatoes.

As George stood smiling, the guest took a bite. The crunchy slice melted in his mouth. He savoured the taste. To George's amazement, the guest congratulated him on his outstanding new dish!

George Crum's "Saratoga Chips" were soon a popular item on the Moon Lodge menu. People started making their own "chips" in kitchens across the country. Then, when the mechanical potato peeling machine was invented in the 1920s, potato chip factories began to produce the treat in bulk. Today the potato chip, George Crum's revenge, ranks as one of the world's favorite snacks.

William Henry Perkin
1856

Sticky Mess, Valuable Solution

Is it possible to improve on nature? Sometimes.

Before the 1800s only the natural hues of minerals, berries and flowers were used to tint fabrics. Then, almost by accident, a young Englishman revolutionized the dye industry.

William Henry Perkin, an eighteen-year-old chemistry assistant, decided to put his Easter holidays of 1856 to good use. He spent his days and evenings experimenting in a small, simple laboratory in his home in England.

His goal? Perkin wanted to produce the chemical quinine from coal tar. Quinine was used by doctors to treat malaria, a common illness in those days. The chemical was in great demand, but could only be obtained from the cinchona tree. If Perkin could make it from coal tar, the medicine would be more readily available.

Perkin set up a series of experiments. He mixed coal tar with various chemicals in test tubes, but none of the mixtures was even close to quinine.

Despite his disappointment, Perkin didn't give up. He continued making careful observations.

One day he noticed a thick black residue at

the bottom of a test tube. When he added alcohol to the sticky mess, it dissolved, and a deep purple liquid appeared. Excited by the exotic color, Perkin forgot about his search for quinine. Instead he tested the brilliant fluid. He found it had all the properties of a dye. He named his lucky find "mauve."

Perkin was fortunate in another way, too. By a curious coincidence, a fashion trend for purple dresses had been started in Europe by Empress Eugenie of France. Perkin was just the man to supply large amounts of the new synthetic dye! He persuaded his father and brother to help him, and in a few months their factory was churning out great quantities of the artificial mauve color.

Was Perkin's success just a bit of luck? Not entirely. If William Henry Perkin hadn't been curious enough to stop for a second look at the black residue in the test tube, he would have overlooked his great discovery. As it was, his interest led to sweeping changes in the dye industry. Now colors could be obtained in greater variety, more cheaply and more easily than ever before.

Eadweard Muybridge
Early 1870s

Pictures in Motion

Imagine this scene ...

The race starts. The horses surge down the track, their pounding hooves leaving a cloud of dust in their wake. The cheering crowd rises to its feet. All eyes follow the thundering horses.

Almost all eyes, that is.

At the front of the track several men aren't paying any attention to the race. Instead they are involved in a heated discussion.

Some of the men maintain that when a horse runs, there's a moment when all its feet are off the ground at the same time. The other men argue that this is impossible.

Every once in a while the men sneak glances at the passing horses as if to study them, but the horses are moving too fast to say for certain how their hooves strike the ground. The argument builds and bets are placed. A great deal of money is at stake. Finally, the group of men hire a scientist to settle the debate.

This interesting scene actually happened at a race track in Sacramento, California, in the early 1870s. The horsemen did hire a scientist, Eadweard Muybridge, to settle the argument. His study of moving horses yielded unexpected results that affect our lives even today.

To settle the debate, Eadweard Muybridge

set up a couple of dozen cameras at regular intervals around the race track. To the shutter of each camera he attached a string that he stretched across the track. As the horse galloped past, the string broke, triggering the shutter and a picture was taken. In the end, Muybridge had dozens of pictures, each a few seconds apart from the others.

Muybridge settled the argument. His pictures proved beyond a shadow of a doubt that there *were* times when a race horse had all four feet off the ground at once.

The winning gamblers must have been pleased, but Muybridge was not finished. He saw possibilities in this study of motion. Eagerly he took thousands of pictures of horses in motion. Then he assembled them in a book he called *The Horse in Motion.*

Muybridge went a step further. He took hundreds of thousands of photographs of all sorts of living things as they moved. His action shots ranged from birds in flight to baseball players running to home plate. Finally he compiled a massive eleven-volume set of books on animal motion.

Even after all his work, Muybridge still wasn't completely satisfied. Although the photographs showed motion split seconds apart, Muybridge hoped to get them even closer in time. Only then would the pictures show motion in its truest form.

He sought help from Thomas Edison, the inventor. As busy as he was, Edison recognized a great idea and in 1888 began to work on the project himself. He found that if Muybridge's photographs were arranged in order, one on top of the other, and then flipped quickly, the passing images seemed to show a horse in motion. If pictures were taken close enough together and then were shown rapidly in sequence, the illusion of motion could be produced!

Edison worked on the moving picture idea for several years. Finally, he developed the kinetoscope, a large wheel containing hundreds of photographs. To use it you looked through an opening and cranked a handle to turn the wheel. As each photograph flipped by it was briefly lit by an electric spark. To the viewer, it looked as though the object in the photographs was really moving!

The kinetoscope was the forerunner of our modern motion picture system. Today, when we watch a movie we are really looking at thousands of individual, but closely spaced, pictures that are projected onto the screen so rapidly that we don't see them as separate images.

Bags, Not Tins

Thomas Sullivan was a coffee and tea importer in New York City at the turn of the century. To promote sales he sent his customers samples of tea leaves in small metal containers. By brewing the loose leaves in boiling water and then straining the tea into cups, his customers could taste several different kinds before ordering a larger supply of their favorites.

Sullivan's business was going well until the price of the small tins skyrocketed in 1904. It was now too expensive to use them for his samples so Sullivan looked for a cheaper way. All of a sudden he had an innovative idea. He would make small bags out of Chinese silk, stuff each with tea and ship the sample packages to his customers.

The samples were an instant hit, but not in the way Sullivan had expected. While Sullivan thought that people would cut open a bag and empty the loose tea into their tea pot, the customers assumed the whole bag was to be brewed! Instead of floating about in the pot, the tea leaves were contained inside the bag, and the messy straining of loose leaves was eliminated.

Orders poured into Sullivan's office. Suddenly, everyone wanted the tea that came in bags instead of tins. Sullivan began to package all his tea in the convenient little bags, and his business prospered. Soon, all his competitors were forced to change their packaging to keep up with the demand for tea bags.

Charles Menches
1904

Favorite Treat

The big event of 1904 was the St. Louis World Fair. The fair included marching bands, art and science displays and fast food stands.

At his booth, Charles Menches sold assorted flavors of ice cream in dishes. Next to him, Ernest Hamwi sold a Middle Eastern dessert, a tasty waffle-like pastry called zalabia.

August was hot. Cool treats were in big demand, and Menches did a booming business selling his ice cream. One scorching day, he sold so much ice cream that by noon he had run out of dishes. Unless he could round up more dishes, he would be forced to close his booth and lose half a day's business.

Menches glanced at his neighbor's booth. Hamwi still had lots of zalabia left. Suddenly, Menches had an idea.

With Hamwi's help he took the thin pastry, rolled it into a cone shape, scooped the ice cream on top and passed it to his customers. They loved the blend of cool and crisp tastes, and Menches' ice cream cone was the hit of the exposition.

In 1912 Frederick A. Bruckman, an inventor from Portland, Oregon, created a machine that made pastry and folded it into cones. By 1920 one-third of all ice cream being consumed in the United States was eaten from cones!

Bibliography

American Heritage. *Men of Science and Invention.* New York: American Heritage Publishing Co. Ltd., 1960.

Asimov, Isaac. *Asimov's Biographical Encyclopedia of Science and Technology.* Garden City: Doubleday & Co. Inc., 1972.

Asimov, Isaac. *Breakthroughs in Science.* Boston: Scholastic Magazine Inc., 1959.

Batten, Mary. *Discovery by Chance.* New York: Funk and Wagnalls, 1968.

Breeden, Robert L., et al. *Those Inventive Americans.* Washington, D.C.: National Geographic Society, 1971.

Brown, J.J. *The Inventors: Great Ideas in Canadian Enterprise.* Toronto: McClelland & Stewart Ltd., 1967.

Campbell, Hannah. *Why Did They Name It . . . ?* New York: Fleet Publishing Co., 1964.

Marsh, James H., ed. *The Canadian Encyclopedia.* Edmonton: Hurtig Publishers, 1988.

Caney, Steven. *Steven Caney's Invention Book.* New York: Workman Publishing Co., 1985.

Crook, Bette, Charles L. Crook, M.D. *Famous Firsts in Medicine.* New York: G.P. Putman's and Sons, 1974.

Crump, Donald J. *Small Inventions That Make a Big Difference.* Washington, D.C.: National Geographic Society, 1984.

De Bono, Edward. *Eureka!* London: Thames and Hudson Ltd., 1974.

D'Estaing, Valarie-Anne Giscard. *The World Almanac Book of Inventions.* New York: World Almanac Publications, 1985.

Dickenson, F.L. *Prairie Wheat* Winnipeg: Canada Grains Council, 1988.

Dietz, David. *All About Great Medical Discoveries.* New York: Random House, 1960.

Epstein, Beryl, Sam Epstein. *Dr. Beaumont and the Man with the Hole in His Stomach.* New York: Coward, McCann and Geoghegan Inc., 1978.

Fletcher Pratt. *All About Famous Inventors and Their Inventions.* New York: Random House, 1955.

Fucini, Josephi J., Susan Franklin. *Entrepreneurs.* Boston: G. K. Hall and Co., 1985.

Gies, Joseph, Frances Gies. *The Ingenious Yankees.* New York: Thomas Y. Crowell Co., 1976.

Hooper, Meredith, *Everyday Inventions.* Sydney: Angus and Robertson Publishing Co. 1972.

Lambert, David, Tony Osmond. *Great Discoveries and Inventions.* London: Orbis Publishing Ltd., 1985.

Land, Barbara. *The Telescope Makers.* New York: Thomas Y. Crowell Co., 1968.

Marks, Geoffrey. *The Amazing Stethoscope.* New York: Julian Messner, 1971.

McGrath, Molly Wade. *Top Sellers USA.* New York: William Morrow & Co. Ltd., 1983.

Meyer, Jerome S. *The World Book of Great Inventions.* Cleveland and New York: The World Publishing Co., 1956.

Nostbakken, J. and Jack Humphrey, *The Canadian*

Inventions Book. Toronto: Greey de Pencier Publications, 1976.

Pine, Tillie S., Joseph Levine. *Scientists and Their Discoveries*. New York: McGraw-Hill Book Co., 1978.

Rowland, K.T. *Eighteenth Century Inventions*. New York: Barnes and Noble, 1974.

Shepherd, Walter. *Great Pioneers of Science*. Great Britain: A. Quick & Co., 1964.

Shipper, Katherine B. *Men of Medicine*. New York: Viking Press, 1957.

Siedel, Frank, James M. Siedel. *Pioneers in Science*. New York: Houghton Mifflin Co., 1968.

Silverberg, Robert. *Scientists and Scoundrels*. New York: Thomas Y. Crowell, 1965.

Sutcliffe, A., A.P.D. Sutcliffe. *Stories from Science: 1*. London: Cambridge University Press, 1962.

Sutcliffe, A., A.P.D. Sutcliffe. *Stories from Science: 2*. London: Cambridge University Press, 1962.

Tharp, Edgar. *Giants of Invention*. New York: Grosset and Dunlap, 1963.

Wulffson, Don L. *Extraordinary Stories Behind the Invention of Ordinary Things*. New York: Lothrop, Lee and Shepard Books, 1981.

Index